A Mirror publication
Marketing Manager: Fergus McKenna
Mirrorpix: David Scripps and Alex Waters
020 7293 3858

Produced by Trinity Mirror Sport Media,
PO BOX 48, Liverpool L69 3EB
0151 227 2000

Executive Editor: Ken Rogers
Senior Editor: Steve Hanrahan
Senior Art Editor: Rick Cooke
Editor: Paul Dove
Compiled and written by: Alan Jewell, William Hughes
Sub Editor: James Cleary
Design: Alison Gilliland, Lisa Critchley, Zoe Bevan

Part of the Mirror Collection
© Published by Trinity Mirror
Images: Mirrorpix
Printed by PCP

CONTENTS

Above: The swagger of success,
on stage in August 1993

Two decades at the top...
and still no stopping them

Twenty years after they set off on the road to stardom, Take That still Rule The World.

November 2010 will bring the release of the group's latest album – and the much anticipated return of Robbie Williams.

Since Gary Barlow, Mark Owen, Howard Donald and Jason Orange reunited to huge acclaim in 2005, there have been rumours and hints aplenty that Robbie would join them.

Fans of the group were finally put out of their misery in July when it was confirmed that all five original members were together again.

An awful lot has happened since five young lads, mostly teenagers, turned up at a nightclub in Manchester 20 years ago to meet a man with a dream. A dream to create a 'boy-band' that would challenge the best that America had to offer.

Within a couple of hours Jason, Howard, Mark, Robbie and Gary were being entertained to a slap up lunch in British Home Stores where Nigel Martin-Smith explained his vision of their future.

Fast-forward six years, during which time they had eight number one records plus another nine hits. Four guys (minus Robbie, who had left in acrimonious circumstances the previous year) announced their break-up to a packed press conference. TV cameras beamed the pictures around the nation and young girls, many overcome with grief, could scarcely believe it. Take That were gone forever…or so it seemed.

Take That were always about the sum of the parts. There were the dancers, Howard Donald and Jason Orange, who were handsome and agile; Mark Owen, the band's very own Oliver; and Robbie Williams, the perfect reincarnation of the Artful Dodger. And then there was Gary Barlow, the special one, who could not dance, was not considered the best looking, but could write pop songs as good as anyone since Lennon and McCartney.

Robbie, having left the band in 1995, tried to forge a solo career but initially he couldn't quite decide whether he was the next one-man Oasis, or whatever it was the public wanted. Gary, having been the musical talent in the band, was tipped for superstardom; Gary even dubbed himself, with a good deal of self-deprecating awareness, 'Mini Elton'. But the best laid plans of record company moguls went badly awry when the Artful Dodger turned into the star and set about conquering the world, leaving Gary to bemoan his loss.

The years rolled by, during which time Howard, Jason and Mark separately tried their hand at being a DJ, an actor and a solo star – with some success. However, it was only Robbie who seemed to have no reins on his popularity. He went from star to superstar while Gary, having been dropped by his record company as a solo artist, began crafting hits for others and enjoyed life as a husband and father.

The fans grew up, got married and harboured a distant glow of being 'Thatters', as the fans of the band called themselves. Take That were destined to become just another in a long list of teenage screams, although one that was more successful than any band since the Beatles.

At the end of 2005 the group (minus Robbie) announced that they were to reform to tour in the early summer of the following year. The tour was hugely successful and the patience of the fans was rewarded when they released a chart-topping single of that name which re-established Take That. The album, Beautiful World, sold almost three million copies in the UK. Since then there have been another two number-one singles, another number-one album and countless awards, plus two more tours including 'The Circus', which was one of the most ambitious live concert productions by any band…ever.

It does not matter whether there are four or five of them, Take That are the greatest British band of the last 20 years – maybe even longer. The ultimate boy-band has become a man-band and it looks like they're Back for Good.

Albums

1992
Take That & Party

1993
Everything Changes

1995
Nobody Else

1996
Greatest Hits

2005
Never Forget – The
Ultimate Collection

2006
Beautiful World

2008
The Circus

2009
The Greatest Day –
Take That Present:
The Circus Live

Above: Performing at the Princess Diana Memorial concert at
Wembley in 2007. Below: Robbie performing at the 2010 Brit Awards

No. 1 singles

1993
Pray

1993
Relight My Fire

1993
Babe

1994
Everything Changes

1994
Sure

1995
Back For Good

1995
Never Forget

1996
How Deep Is Your Love

2006
Patience

2007
Shine

2008
Greatest Day

THE BOYS MAKE A NOISE

AFTER THE PHENOMENAL SUCCESS ENJOYED BY NEW KIDS ON THE BLOCK, MANCHESTER-BASED MUSIC MANAGER NIGEL MARTIN-SMITH DECIDED TO SET UP A BRITISH VERSION OF THE BOY-BAND. AFTER A DIFFICULT START, THEY ECLIPSED ANYTHING THAT HAD GONE BEFORE

MOST NAUSEATING POP NEWCOMER

1 Dannii Minogue
2 Chesney Hawkes
3 Vic Reeves
4 Right Said Fred
5 Marky Mark
6 Color Me Badd
7 Vanilla Ice
8 Crystal Waters
9 Carter USM
10 Take That

Take That find heaven: Flops drove band to breaking point

Tuesday, August 11, 1992

Teen stars Take That are thanking their lucky stars after finally finding chart success following a series of flops.

The heart-throb band, now at No. 12 with new single 'I Found Heaven', were all set to split up after three consecutive singles bombed.

Then came 'It Only Takes A Minute'. It hit the top 10 in May and saved the day. Gary Barlow, singer with the Manchester-based five-piece, whose raunchy stage act sends female fans wild, reveals: "We talked very seriously about splitting up before that song came out. We would not have been able to carry on if it had been a flop.

"You wouldn't believe how happy we were that the record was a hit."

Band-mate Robbie Williams, 18, adds: "I was very worried about our future. I was convinced I'd have to forget about a pop career and go back to college.

"Luckily, the fans started to get behind us."

No sex please, we're ambitious

Monday, August 17, 1992

Pop heart-throbs Take That have banned sex for a year in a bid for superstardom.

The Manchester pin-ups are petrified that nookie could ruin their careers.

The five-piece band – this week at No. 17 with 'I Found Heaven' – are driving girls wild with their good looks and raunchy dance routines.

But 21-year-old singer Jason Orange says: "We all vowed to put all our energies into our music.

"Our manager said if we want to be the best band around, girls would distract us.

"He has seen bands go off the rails because they went girl-mad.

"We know it will be hard because we like girls so much. But it's for the best."

Sex-crazy fans try all the tricks, like hiding in their hotel rooms, to meet the group.

Mark Owen, 20, says: "We are now being rushed out of gigs to avoid all temptation.

"We miss girls but a relationship would be very unfair.

"With our hectic lifestyle any girlfriends would probably see more of us in magazines than in the flesh."

Left and above: Group photographs from 1991 and 1992 showing Robbie, Jason, Mark, Gary and Howard as fresh-faced young lads. On the opposite page, a cutting from the Daily Mirror after they were voted 10th most nauseating pop newcomer in 1991

Beat that!
Geordie gals go crazy
for fantastic five

Wednesday, November 4, 1992

Take That, critics! The band they said would never make it big took Newcastle by storm at the start of their blockbusting British tour.

The pop world's latest teen sensation drove 2,000 girl fans wild with 80 minutes of raunchy high energy in the City Hall.

There were at most just six blokes in the audience to share the shrieking, shaking female frenzy as Take That gave them their all.

The last time a British band caused such hysteria was at the height of Brosmania.

But not everybody's a fan, as band heart-throb Gary Barlow explained after the concert.

He had narrowly escaped a beating when he was set upon as he waited alone at a motorway service station.

"The rest of the band were late and these six thugs surrounded me, pushing and swearing. I thought I was going to get my head kicked in."

Luckily blond Gary was rescued by the arrival of the band.

As teen idols go, the Manchester five-piece have a lot to offer. They have better songs than Bros, are hunkier than New Kids On The Block and more dynamic than Jason Donovan.

Their dance routines are breathtaking and they pen fine pop songs – like their current ballad 'A Million Love Songs'.

Excited fan Michelle Langwell, 15, summed it up:

"They've got great songs, they're canny and they're reet horny."

* Take That have won many gay fans – and they're delighted. Singer Jason Orange says: "We are happy to perform at gay clubs. I'm really proud of our gay following. We get a lot of fan letters from men and I love reading them."

Band-mate Robbie Williams adds: "It's very flattering that both sexes fancy us."

* JASON ORANGE has a crush on Kylie Minogue…HOWARD DONALD has a pet snake called Sid…ROBBIE WILLIAMS says he's never been in love…GARY BARLOW'S nickname at school was Goose. To this day he doesn't know why…MARK OWEN came bottom of the class in German.

* Jason Orange thought he was out of the tour after a nasty accident while rehearsing.

The Mohican-cropped star pulled a ligament during a frenzied dance routine.

He says: "I was in agony. I was rushed to a doctor who told me I had to stop dancing. If not, I was risking permanent injury.

"So I rested completely, had my knee bound up and was given some tablets and injections.

"A few days before the first show I was given the all-clear. I was still in pain at Newcastle but the sheer excitement and adrenaline of performing made me forget all about any injury."

ALBUM REVIEW

Take That And Party:
Take That

IT hasn't been easy for Take That to break into the big time. Now their debut album could change all that. Among the tracks that will get teens' hearts beating are the title track, I Found Heaven and the smoochy ballad A Million Love Songs.

Left: A positive review from the Mirror in August 1992 predicts that success is in store for the boys

With Jordan Knight from New Kids On The Block, the group that inspired the formation of Take That

TAKE TWO

The boys were given an award by the British Dental Association for keeping their teeth pearly white.

Performing on stage in November

RICK SKY'S THE LIMIT SPECIAL ON THE SMASH HITS AWARDS

VICTORS: Take That dancing with joy

TAKE THAT!
We're the new kids at the top

FULL MARK Marky's dance act was voted the best around by the young pop lovers

OFF BEAT Richard Fairbrass was a wow as he performed in a fetching little black outfit

KYLIE CANED

Miss Minogue was voted an unfanciable woman and second worst female singer

POP sensations Take That hit their rivals for SEVEN in yesterday's Smash Hits awards.

The Manchester group picked up two more top spots than the five scooped last year by America's New Kids On The Block.

This time the Kids came away without a single major award. Instead, teeny fans voted them the **WORST** band of the year.

Take That, presently at No 9 with Could It Be Magic, set a record with their seven awards.

Among their prizes were Best Group, Best Single, Best LP and Best Video.

Jubilant Mark Owen said after the ceremony in London: "This time last year we were wondering if we'd ever make it. I can't believe this has happened to us. It's wonderful."

Hand

New Kids' Jordan Knight was on hand to see his band's humiliation — he co-hosted the show with Radio One DJ Simon Mayo.

The US band were not alone. Kylie Minogue and Jason Donovan were also destroyed by the young voters.

Kylie failed to get an award and was voted second worst female singer, second least fanciable woman and third worst dressed star.

Jason Donovan was voted the world's worst male singer — but confus-

Seven prizes for Brit band

BLOCKED OFF: New Kids are the worst band

ingly scraped the title of second best too.

Best male solo singer was Michael Jackson.

Other stars on the teens' hate list were Kylie's sister Dannii who was voted Worst Female Singer, Melissa Bell who was voted worst actress and TV's Spender, Jimmy Nail, who won the Least Fanciable Male section.

Fans were split over Madonna. They voted her Best Female Singer and Worst Film Actress.

And she topped the polls for both **MOST** and **LEAST** Fanciable Female.

Premier John Major also made his mark. The magazine's readers voted him Villain Of The Year.

Two other Tories also

got the order of the boot. Chancellor Norman Lamont came sixth, one place ahead of David Mellor.

The much hyped Batman Returns was voted the worst film.

Best TV programme was Australian soap Home and Away while Eldorado was voted the worst.

Chart-topping group The Shamen were voted best new act.

Sip

Sprinter Linford Christie was the teens' hero of the year. When he received his gong he told a cheering audience that he "was going to run even faster next year."

Marky Mark, who won the Best Dance Act of the year, took a shine to Kylie Minogue backstage and asked her back to his hotel to sip some champagne.

Shakespear's Sister Marcie Detroit just loved the bald bonce of Right Said Fred's Richard Fairbrass and gave it some loving caresses in the dressing room.

SKY'S THE LIMIT ● See Page 15

Above: An early example of fans' adoration during one of the group's first major tours

Above: The boys go through a dance routine. On the opposite page, the Mirror reports on Take That's record seven awards at the Smash Hits Poll Winners Party

1992

FEBRUARY 8
Once You've Tasted Love reaches 47 in the charts

JUNE
At a record signing in Stoke-on-Trent, Take That hear that It Only Takes A Minute made it to 25 on the midweek chart. When the full charts were announced it had moved up to 16

JUNE
Radio One Roadshow performance at Alton Towers

AUGUST 16
I Found Heaven reaches 15 and stays on the chart for six weeks

SEPTEMBER 5
The debut album Take That & Party enters the album chart at number 5. It peaks at 2 and stays on the chart for 73 weeks. Meanwhile, the band embark on more in-store record signings – 2,000 turn up in Glasgow, 3,000 in London and 5,000 in Manchester. They have to be smuggled out of the building and HMV cancel the remaining signings for safety reasons

OCTOBER 10
A Million Love Songs enters the UK singles chart. It makes number 7

NOVEMBER 2
The band kick off their Take That & Party tour at Newcastle City Hall

DECEMBER 12
A cover of the Barry Manilow track Could It Be Magic enters the UK singles chart. It makes number 3

DECEMBER
Take That sweep the board at the Smash Hits Poll Winners Party, winning seven awards including Best Band in The World, Best Single and Best Album

HITTING THE TOP

IN 1993 TAKE THAT RELEASED THE 'EVERYTHING CHANGES' ALBUM AND ENJOYED THEIR FIRST NUMBER ONE SINGLE WITH 'PRAY' IN JULY. THEY HAD TWO MORE CHART-TOPPERS BEFORE THE END OF THE YEAR AS THE GROUP WENT FROM BOY-BAND TO CULTURAL PHENOMENON

Promoting an official book at Planet Hollywood in June

Banned from love

Thursday, April 29, 1993

Forget it, girls. You may fancy them like mad, but pop's heart-throb sensations aren't up for grabs.

Well, actually, they are up for grabs, but falling in love is out of the question.

Who says so? Take That's boss. And he's spelt it out by cracking down on the lads with a two-year love ban.

"Flings and flirtations are fine," manager Nigel Martin-Smith has told Mark, Howard, Robbie, Jason and Gary. "But the real thing – sorry, no.

"Some people say it's not natural for guys their age not to have girlfriends," Nigel admits.

"I have never insisted they behave like monks. But there's no room in their lives for heavy, serious relationships."

Nigel's biggest fear is that girlfriends could become more important to the boys than the band itself. And that steady relationships could prove a huge turn-off for Take That fans.

Hardest hit by the love ban is Howard Donald, who admits: "I fall in love very deeply and I think that to be in a relationship and to spend so much time away would be unfair for both of us.

"The way things are now, if I was to meet a girl, I would never find out if she was the right one because I wouldn't be able to spend enough time with her."

1993

With Mr
Blobby, who
prevented the
group from
having a
Christmas
number one by
knocking
'Babe' off the
top of the
charts

1993

14

FEBRUARY 20
Why Can't I Wake Up With You enters the UK singles chart and reaches number 2

MAY
The band record Pray. A promotional trip to the USA follows with the video shot in Acapulco

JUNE 28
The band play at the Capital Radio Roadshow at Crystal Palace where 30,000 fans turn up

JULY 5
Pray is released

JULY
Take That begin rehearsals in Wales for their forthcoming Summer of Love tour

How a top band stumbled on their way to stardom

Monday, July 12, 1993

Take That are the biggest heart-throbs Britain has seen for years – but the band nearly never happened.

Because it was a total fluke that Gary Barlow, Mark Owen, Jason Orange, Robbie Williams and Howard Donald – currently at No. 1 with Pray – ever came together.

Jason was reluctant to leave the security of his Manchester City Council works department job.

Robbie wanted to be an actor and drama teacher. Howard had never considered quitting his £40-a-week job as a car spray painter.

And Mark dreamed of becoming a professional footballer – he even trialled for Manchester United.

Only Gary Barlow wanted to be a pop singer, something he had pursued since the age of 13.

Hunky Jason took a lot of persuading to join up when approached by manager Nigel Martin-Smith, who dreamed of creating the perfect pop group.

Jason and partner Neil McCartney were happy enough with their success as a dance act on the Hitman and Her ITV show.

Says Jason, a former painter and decorator: "I was young and daft then, and I just wanted to enjoy myself. I didn't particularly fancy the idea of being in a band." Recalls Martin-Smith: "Jason's friend Neil approached me and told me they were looking for a manager.

"I thought Jason had star quality. But he didn't really want to know about being in a pop group. I couldn't believe how cool he was."

Youngest band member Robbie wasn't keen either. His burning ambition was to be an actor and later to teach drama.

"My mum really wanted me to go to college. I would have liked to do drama at university."

Then he met Martin-Smith while still at school. "I was in the fifth year when I auditioned for Nigel," says Robbie.

No one was more surprised than him when he beat off hundreds of other young hopefuls in a gruelling audition to become Take That's fifth member. Admits Robbie: "I'd almost forgotten about the audition. I was blown away when I arrived home and my mum said she had some good news. She told me Nigel had been on the phone and I was in the group. I couldn't believe it, I felt ecstatic."

As a teenager, Mark Owen was shattered when he failed trials for Manchester United and Rochdale. Says Mark: "I lived for football. It was my life. I was heartbroken."

It was a chance meeting with Gary Barlow that changed his life. He graduated from carrying Gary's keyboards and amps to become a fully-fledged band member.

Before finding fame, Howard Donald, the group's oldest member, worked as a vehicle painter, earning a princely sum of £40 a week.

He was happy just dancing the night away in local clubs before running into Jason. He admits: "Never in a million years did I think I would do something like this."

Only Gary Barlow had plans for a pop career. But even Gary, the first of the band to be snapped up by Martin-Smith, was off-key.

Says Martin-Smith: "Gary wanted to be a solo artist, but I saw him as part of a group.

"He wasn't convinced at first – but in the end he came round to my way of thinking."

A rest and a refreshing drink as their schedule becomes ever more hectic. On the opposite page, they pose with Manchester United captain Bryan Robson and the Premier League trophy at Old Trafford

15

Pointing the way forward
during the summer tour

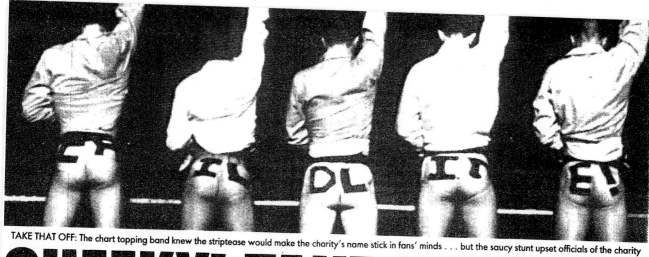

TAKE THAT OFF: The chart topping band knew the striptease would make the charity's name stick in fans' minds . . . but the saucy stunt upset officials of the charity

CHEEKY! TAKE THAT ARE BOTTOM OF THE POPS

18

Jason Orange on stage at the NEC in Birmingham. Above, some bare-faced cheek causes controversy

TAKE TWO

Jason Orange admitted to being smitten with his French teacher when he was at school. He said: "I had a huge crush on Miss Cadwell. She was very well developed and when she had her top button undone, it would drive me mad. I was totally obsessed with her. Whenever she asked me a question, I would flush, go blank and look at her wide-eyed."

Cheeky! Take That are bottom of the pops

Monday, August 16, 1993

Teen idols Take That got a dressing down – for staging a saucy striptease at a kids' charity concert.

The heart-throb band – who recently hit No. 1 with their single 'Pray' – dropped their trousers in front of 10,000 fans, then turned to reveal the word Childline across their undies.

Childline chiefs were told they performed the stunt to give the charity maximum publicity.

But they were said to be upset by it, even though the weekend concert raised a much-needed £60,000 for the ailing charity – started by TV star Esther Rantzen.

Take That's singer Gary Barlow defended the strip.

He said: "We wanted to give Childline the maximum amount of publicity we could.

"And we felt that this was a great, fun way of doing it. We knew that would keep the word in every fan's mind."

Fellow band member Mark Owen said: "Childline is a great charity and we are only too happy to help.

"It's the kids who put us where we are today and it's nice to give something back."

A spokesman for the group said: "I have heard that Childline weren't too happy about the act.

"But it's Take That's show and they wanted it as part of their performance."

In concert in Manchester in July

Standing together during the show at the Birmingham NEC

19

Another date at the NEC in Birmingham, this time in November

1993

JULY 12
Pray enters the UK singles chart and goes on to become the band's first number 1 single

JULY 20
Start a run of seven consecutive nights of concerts at the Manchester G-Mex

END OF AUGUST
The video for Relight My Fire is recorded at London's Ministry of Sound club

SEPTEMBER
Promotional trip to Japan

SEPTEMBER 23
Take That perform Relight My Fire on Top Of The Pops

OCTOBER 9
Relight My Fire enters the UK singles chart. It becomes their second number 1 and stays on the chart for 14 weeks

Go get 'em girls!

Thursday, October 7, 1993

It's the news millions of young girls have been longing to hear – Take That's two-year ban on girlfriends is officially over.

But before lovelorn fans beg the five heart-throbs, now at number one with 'Relight My Fire', to make them a potential Mrs Take That, there's something they should know.

The boys – Gary Barlow, Mark Owen, Robbie Williams, Jason Orange and Howard Donald – are going to extend the ban voluntarily when they begin their British tour next month.

"Originally the no girlfriends rule was our manager's idea," says Gary, 22.

"He didn't mind us making love – he didn't want us to be monks – but he thought that if we had regular girlfriends it would be a big distraction to our career.

"He reasoned that if we fell madly in love, the group would start to take second place to our girlfriends and he asked us if we wanted that to happen.

"The group is very important to us and we wanted it to succeed. So we agreed to do as he said."

A spot of pole
dancing from Robbie

THAT'S more like it. Jason, second from left, as he usually is.

TAKE THAT OFF!

WHO'S 'THAT' GIRL? Teen idol Jason Orange stuns thousands of girl fans with his peroxide wig and polka-dot dress.

Pictures by DUNCAN RABAN and JUSTIN THOMAS

By RICK SKY

Jason in drag act shocker

THIS IS Take That star Jason Orange proving he's a smash hit – as a girl.

The teen pop idol even fooled his screaming female fans as he suddenly appeared as a cross between Madonna and Marilyn Monroe at the opening gig of the group's British tour.

Dressed in a fetching polka-dot dress, his peroxide wig adorned with a pretty bow, the outrageous singer did a smoochy dance on stage with fellow band-member Howard Donald.

And he did it so well that many of the fans in the audience thought there was a new girl in the group.

They stared open-mouthed as Jason jived with Howard to a number from Grease.

Afterwards Jason said: "It was my idea. I thought it would be great fun and it was."

"I have never dressed up in drag before and fancied doing something a little bit zany.

"I think I looked a picture, though it was hard to remember to do the woman's steps in the dance."

Rumours

The band have always denied the gay rumours that have circulated after they were banned from having girlfriends for two years by their manager.

Jason recently admitted that he is sometimes attracted to other guys. "A man can turn me on as much as a woman, but not necessarily in a sexual way," he said.

But it was the girls who were swooning at the gig in Bournemouth – the first of the group's 21 British concerts.

More than 200 hysterical fans fainted during the sparkling two-hour show.

Ambulancemen and security guards were carting them out of the hall by the dozen as the lads on stage went through their paces.

The group, now Britain's hottest pop property, treated the 4,000-strong audience to some of their biggest hits, including It Only Takes A Minute, Why Can't I Wake Up With You, Pray, and their recent number one smash Re-Light My Fire.

Shorts

There were seven costume changes which included trench coats and trilbys, hooded monk's habits as well as the regulation white T-shirts and jeans.

But in the end it was Jason again who stole the show.

He changed out of his dress . . . into a see-through yellow top and black leather shorts.

Mirror PICTURE EXCLUSIVE

NEWS AT TEN STAYS AT TEN

NEWS at Ten is staying put. ITV chiefs who wanted to move it have backed down after protests led by Premier John Major.

"It's at 10pm for the foreseeable future," said ITV network director Marcus Plantin. He hinted two months ago the timing could change.

Mr Major then wrote to Sir

By GORDON HAY

George Russell, chairman of ITV watchdog the ITC, saying a switch would greatly undermine competition between news channels.

Mr Plantin announced the climbdown as ITV revealed its

£186 million winter schedule, which includes eight new series.

Royal stories are two highlights. One is The House of Windsor, a below-stairs look at Buckingham Palace, and another is a cartoon based on the Duchess of York's Budgie The Helicopter stories.

David Jason is returning to his detective role in A Touch of Frost and Leslie Grantham will star as an undercover cop in a new show, 99-1.

Joanna Lumley joins the ITV line-up playing an aristocrat fallen on hard times in Class Act.

Another highlight is TV's Mr Grumpy, Richard Wilson, and Jan Francis in the series Under the Hammer, set in the world of international auctions.

Coronation Street's Roy Barraclough teams up with Dora Bryan for a northern sitcom, Mother's Ruin.

Mirror saves kids' Rainbow

AXED TV favourite Rainbow is back – thanks to the Mirror.

ITV chiefs have bowed to pressure and revived the hit series – with one difference.

Presenter Geoffrey Hayes, who hosted the show along with Zippy and Bungle Bear, will be replaced by a new female

puppet called Cleo. The U-turn comes after thousands of viewers wrote in protest following the Mirror's revelation that the 20-year programme was to be scrapped.

PALS: Geoff & Zippy

23

Above: Going through their routines while in concert at Whitley Bay Ice Rink in December, the last date of the Everything Changes tour. On the opposite page, the Mirror reports on Jason Orange dressing up in drag during a show in Bournemouth

Gary Barlow holds
centre-stage

24

1993

OCTOBER 23
Everything Changes enters the album chart. It makes number 1 and stays on the chart for 78 weeks

NOVEMBER 8
The band start their Everything Changes tour in Bournemouth. The tour takes in 21 dates

DECEMBER 18
Babe enters the UK singles chart and becomes the band's third successive chart topper

DECEMBER
At the Smash Hits Poll Winners Party, Take That win everything in sight!

PAGE 28   DAILY MIRROR, Tuesday, December 21, 1993   LNS

THE EDGE
By RICK SKY

BEST MALE SOLO ARTIST
Meat Loaf
George Michael
Michael Jackson
Phil Collins
Prince
Michael Bolton
Bryan Adams
Elton John
Kenny Thomas
Lenny Kravitz

BEST FEMALE SOLO ARTIST
Dina Carroll
Whitney Houston
Mariah Carey
Madonna
Janet Jackson
Gabrielle
Lisa Stansfield
Bjork
Annie Lennox
Tina Turner

BEST GROUP
Take That
U2
M People
REM
Pet Shop Boys
Guns N' Roses
Wet Wet Wet
Simply Red
UB40
Crowded House

WORST GROUP
Take That
E17
Bad Boys Inc
Two Unlimited
New Kids On the Block
Right Said Fred
Worlds Apart
U2
Guns N' Roses
Bee Gees

BEST LP
Everything Changes
        Take That
Bat Out Of Hell II
        Meat Loaf
The Bodyguard
So Far So Good
        Bryan Adams
Take That And Party
        Take That

BEST SINGLE
I'd Do Anything For Love
        Meat Loaf
Pray   Take That
Relight My Fire Take That
I Will Always Love You
        Whitney Houston
Don't Be A Stranger
        Dina Carroll

TAKE THAT VOTED BEST AND WORST

THE Edge had its say about who it loved and loathed all year, and now it's our turn to listen to YOU.

Today we print the results of our Edge poll for which we had thousands of entries.

And what a revealing poll it was. Pop's number one teen band Take That romped home, winning four categories.

Giving the Manchester lads a run for their money was heavyweight rocker Meat Loaf with three awards and Dina Carroll with two.

Take That won the best group and album sections, while the band's Mark Owen won the most fanciable person category.

They would have also won the best pop single and video awards but their fans' votes were split between three records in both sections.

GROUP'S FOUR: Take That proved they are the hottest thing in Britain, winning four categories

Tops and flops of 93

Surprise

Take That proved they have their fair share of enemies as well when they topped the worst group section.

Pop's real life Mr Blobby, American Meat Loaf, won best solo male singer, and his hit I'd Do Anything For Love won

best single and video. The biggest surprise was Dina Carroll winning the best female singer section over superstars such as Madonna and Whitney Houston.

Dina has raced to the top of your affections in lightning time, as proved by the fact that she also scooped the best newcomer award. When

it comes to who you prefer to play your favourite sounds on the radio, the award deservedly went to Britain's most inventive DJ – Radio One's Steve Wright.

Britain's current chart-topper Mr Blobby failed to win any awards, despite figuring in several sections, but his boss Noel Edmonds was a winner.

Romped

His sparkling show Noel's House Party won your vote as TV's best programme.

Funnyman Michael Barrymore was your favourite TV personality, while Coronation Street's Reg Holdsworth romped home as your top soap character.

The side-splitting John Smith's Bitter telly ad

with Jack Dee was the best commercial. But Aussie soap Neighbours has really lost favour.

Once one of TV's most loved shows, Edge readers said it was the worst show in Britain.

Your favourite film featured a lot of old dinosaurs – Steven Spielberg's Jurassic Park. Tom

Cruise and Whoopi Goldberg were voted your number one film stars.

In the royal stakes, the disintegration of Prince Charles and Princess Diana's marriage was uppermost in your mind. Edge readers voted Diana as the most loved Royal and Charles as the least popular.

MR WRIGHT: DJ Steve

MR WRONG: Blobby

FRESH STAR: Dina

BIG TIME: Meat Loaf

BEST TV SHOW
Noel's House Party
Coronation Street
Big Breakfast
EastEnders
Soldier Soldier
Brookside
Red Dwarf
One Foot In The Grave
Absolutely Fabulous
Cracker

BEST SOAP STAR
Reg Holdsworth
Bet Lynch
Shane (Home And Away)
Barry Grant
Raquel Wolstenhulme
Frank Butcher
Vera Duckworth
Brad Willis
Jack Duckworth

BEST FILM
Jurassic Park
The Fugitive
The Bodyguard
Indecent Proposal
Sleepless In Seattle
In The Line Of Fire
Demolition Man
A Few Good Men
Sister Act
Unforgiven

BEST ACTOR
Tom Cruise
Kevin Costner
Harrison Ford
Mel Gibson
Clint Eastwood
Arnold Schwarzenegger
Sylvester Stallone
Robert De Niro
Jeff Goldblum
Anthony Hopkins

BEST ACTRESS
Whoopi Goldberg
Michelle Pfeiffer
Demi Moore
Sharon Stone
Meg Ryan
Julia Roberts
Kim Basinger
Jodie Foster
Goldie Hawn
Emma Thompson

BEST DJ
Steve Wright
Bruno Brookes
Simon Mayo
Danny Baker
Chris Tarrant
Neil Fox
Simon Bates
John Peel
Pat Sharp
Dave Lee Travis

Above: Performing 'Relight My Fire' with Lulu during the Smash Hits Poll Winners Party at Wembley Arena. At the top of the page, the group's popularity is clear with Mirror readers

Scenes of Take That fan hysteria, including young girls waiting for a Manchester performance, an autograph session and overnight queues as tickets go on sale for a concert in Glasgow

26

CONQUERING EUROPE

THE GROUP CONTINUED TO BECOME BIGGER AND BIGGER AS HIT FOLLOWED HIT AND AWARD FOLLOWED AWARD. THEIR SHOWS IN BRITAIN HAD BEEN A HUGE SUCCESS – NOW THEY BROADENED THEIR HORIZONS BY EMBARKING ON A MONEY-SPINNING EUROPEAN TOUR

Posing in striking blue suits at the 1994 Brit Awards. On the opposite page, Gary pictured as a 14-year-old entertainer

Take a hike

Thursday, February 3, 1994

Robbie Williams's mum has told the hordes of Take That fans who have been besieging the family home to sling their hook.

Theresa Williams, fed up with the army of lovesick girls, has pinned a note to the front door telling them to leave her in peace.

The note, written in blue felt tip, reads: "Dear fans, thanks for calling. I am sorry, but Rob isn't home now. In fact, he has had to spend some time away because he is not getting any privacy.

"It would be very considerate of you if you would not knock and disturb us. With love and thanks, Mrs Williams."

The Take That heart-throb has now been forced to move out of the Tunstall, Stoke-on-Trent home into the nearby village of Hanchurch.

Robbie's sister, Sally, says: "It is my mum who suffers the most because Robbie and I do not live here all the time.

"Fans never stop knocking on the door and mum never gets any peace."

TAKE THAT.. WHO'S THAT?

WHO'S this fresh-faced 14-year-old lad posing with his childhood sweetheart?

By RACHEL MURPHY and RICK SKY

His winning smile looks familiar — but you'd never guess he went on to take the pop world by storm.

Yesterday the girl by his side solved the mystery when we asked 'Who's that?'

It's none other than Take That's heart throb lead singer Gary Barlow and the girl is Heather Woodall, now a 22 year old design student, who still sees Gary.

Said Heather: "I still keep in touch with Gary regularly, in fact I phoned him yesterday. There's no romance any more - we're just good friends.

"We went out for quite a long time. He was my first boyfriend and we dreamed of making the big-time."

Gary was 12 when he met 11- year-old Heather in her home town of Frodsham, Cheshire. Two years later they formed Gary's first group, a duo called Karisma, and in our photo they receive their winning cheque from a talent contest.

STAR: Singer Gary

TAKE THAT: Gary Barlow and Heather Woodall show their early talent

TAKE TWO

Panini sticker albums are generally associated with football fans but the Italian company also produced a 32-page Take That album with 144 stickers to collect.

That'll do nicely!

Monday, March 28, 1994

Some bands who have tasted the kind of phenomenal success Take That have experienced might be content to put up their feet and start spending their hard-earned cash.

But Take That don't just want to be Britain's biggest teen band, they want to conquer the world too – and the boys have no intention of hanging up their mikes just yet.

This year they embark on their biggest ever British tour, playing 36 dates to almost 400,000 fans.

The tour has already been a staggering success. When the first 16 dates were announced they sold out in hours, and further dates had to be added.

Last Thursday they began a European tour which will see them play to another 100,000 fans in Germany, Holland and Sweden among others.

Those two jaunts alone will rake in £12 million from ticket sales and the slick merchandising surrounding the band.

Says the group's Gary Barlow: "The international work is hard and can be very tiring.

"It's non-stop. But once you're on stage and you hear the cheers it makes it all worth it.

"Before our European tour we played a one-off in Germany and the crowd went mad.

"But this tour is bigger than anything we've done in Europe before so, of course, we'll be nervous."

Over the last few months the band has been surrounded by rumours.

One claimed that Gary Barlow was set to leave the hit-making fivesome.

But Gary says: "That's rubbish. I'm not leaving.

"A lot of people have tried to put the boot into us saying that we wouldn't last.

"We proved them wrong. Fans shouldn't worry, this band will be around for a long time."

The boys are particularly devoted to their countless fans.

Recently some fans phoned this column complaining that the band are no longer friendly.

Says Gary: "Obviously things change but the fans mean more than anything. Without them we wouldn't be here."

The band's new single 'Everything Changes', released today, will carry on their successful chart run.

Their last three singles 'Pray', 'Relight My Fire' and 'Babe' went straight to number one.

The song is backed by the Beatles medley which they performed at the Brit Awards.

Adds Gary: "People thought we were comparing ourselves to the Beatles but we weren't.

"We do think we have something in common though. They were a band who had fun and that's what we've always tried to do."

Take That to ape Monkees: BBC boss offers zany sitcom

Wednesday, June 1, 1994

Britain's TV bosses are fighting a big-money battle to launch Take That's television career.

The chart-topping stars have been flooded with offers to star in their own television show since hitting the pop jackpot.

And now BBC1 boss Alan Yentob wants the fab five to star in a sitcom similar to 'The Monkees' – the hit Sixties TV show that starred the crazy American pop heart-throbs.

Says a source close to the band: "Alan Yentob wanted to have the boys starring in their own TV show.

"He thinks they've got a great comic touch and could pull in viewers with a zany Monkees-type show.

"The last we heard he was setting up a series of meetings with the group's manager Nigel Martin-Smith."

Last night the band's Gary Barlow said all the offers had been put on hold.

Says Gary: "Just about every channel has been offering us a TV show. Maybe we will do one, maybe we won't. We haven't made any decisions yet. It is all very flattering.

"But first and foremost we are a music act, not TV presenters or comedy stars."

A spokesman for BBC1 controller Yentob, Andrew Skinner, confirmed that an idea for a show featuring the band was being considered.

TAKE TWO

Gary Barlow attended the Ivor Novello awards while wearing a Versace gold suit featuring gold safety pins, the male version of actress Elizabeth Hurley's famous dress. The millionaire singer admitted he had only borrowed the outfit for the event as he was too stingy to spend £4,000 on it.

30

Above: Excited fans outside the SECC, Glasgow in August for the Pops Tour

31

An Orange tongue. Jason on
stage at the NEC in
Birmingham in September

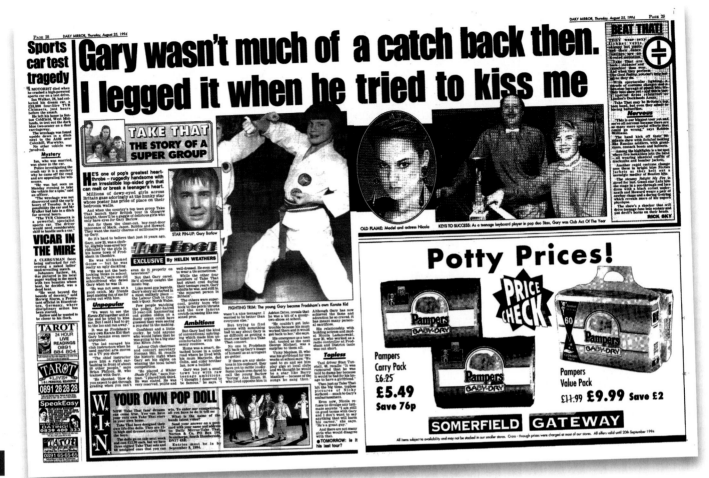

Gary wasn't much of a catch back then.
I legged it when he tried to kiss me

Thursday, August 25, 1994

He's one of pop's greatest heart-throbs – ruggedly handsome with an irresistible lop-sided grin that can melt or break a teenager's heart.

Millions of dewy-eyed girls across Britain gaze adoringly at the hunky star whose poster has pride of place on their bedroom walls.

And when the country's top teen group Take That launch their British tour in Glasgow tonight, there'll be a gaggle of delirious girls who only have eyes for Gary Barlow.

Gary, now 23, was a chubby, slightly boss-eyed boy ridiculed by the girls in his home town of Frodsham in Cheshire.

He was nicknamed Goose – but he was really an ugly duckling.

"He was not the best-looking bloke in school, far from it," says one old schoolfriend who dated Gary when he was 12.

"He was not seen as a good catch. My friends kept making fun of me for going out with him.

"We went to see Karate Kid together and at the end he tried to kiss me. But I said I had to go to the loo and ran away."

It was as Frodsham's very own Karate Kid that Gary became even more unpopular.

The lad enraged his club instructors when he used martial arts moves on a TV pop show.

"The chief instructor gave him a right ear-bashing in front of about 50 other people," says Brian Philcox, 39, who trained with Gary.

He shouted: "How do you expect to get through grading when you can't even do it properly on television?"

Not that Gary cared. He'd already caught the music bug.

Like most pop legends, Gary's story all started in a most unlikely place – the Labour Club in Connah's Quay, North Wales.

Few people watching the podgy, fair-haired 12-year-old hammering out golden oldies on a dusty organ could have guessed they were seeing a pop star in the making.

Confident and a little cocky, he told anyone who would listen that he was going to be a big star like Elton John.

Labour Club chairman and concert secretary Norman Hill, 63, recalls the historic night when Gary set his sights on winning the local talent competition.

"He played 'A Whiter Shade Of Pale'," says Norman. "I placed him third. He was elated. He was very reserved, polite and well dressed. He even used to wear a tie sometimes."

While the other four members of Take That had street cred during their teenage years, Gary admits that he was, and still is, "the squarest person in Britain".

The others were super-cool, pretty boys who took the pelvic thrusts and the now famous crotch-caressing like seasoned pros.

But Gary had the kind of conventional upbringing which made him uncomfortable with the saucy routines.

Home was a smart, detached house in a quiet road where he lived with his mum Marjorie, dad Colin, and older brother Ian, now a builder.

Gary was just a small town boy with raw teenage ambitions.

"I thought I deserved to be famous," he says. "I wasn't a nice teenager. I wanted to be better than everyone else."

But trying to find anyone with something bad to say about Gary is as difficult

Gary and Mark during one of the Birmingham NEC shows

33

TAKE TWO

It was estimated that if fans bought every piece of official Take That merchandise, it would cost them £1,300. The gear ranged from a £1 button badge to an official tour jacket which cost £70.

as getting a front-row ticket to a Take That concert. No-one will back-up Gary's image of himself as an arrogant go-getter.

If there are any skeletons in his cupboard, they have yet to rattle loudly. Some locals even dared to call the young Barlow "boring". Ann Ellam, 23, who lived opposite him in Ashton Drive, reveals that he was a bit of a goody-two-shoes at school.

"He couldn't get into trouble because his mum worked there and it would get back to her," she says.

His emergence as a teen idol, touted as the next George Michael, was a surprise to them all.

Vicky Maplass, 23, who was his girlfriend for two weeks at school says: "We used to go and see him play gigs at local clubs and we thought he would be a star like Barry Manilow because of the songs he sang then."

Although Gary has now achieved the fame and adoration he so craved, it has meant many personal sacrifices.

His relationship with budding actress and model Nicola Ladanowski, now 20, who worked as a radio controller at Frodsham and District taxis was cut short.

Taxi driver Stan Tunstall, 48, recalls: "It was rumoured that he was told to dump her because it would be bad for his image to have a girlfriend."

Then just as Take That hit the big time, topless pictures of Nicky surfaced – much to Gary's embarrassment.

Even now, Nicola refuses to divulge any intimate secrets: "I am still on good terms with Gary and I don't want to say anything that will harm his career," she says. "He's a great guy."

And there are not many girls who would disagree with that.

TAKE THAT
20 YEARS OF HITS AND SPLITS

1994

FEBRUARY
Take That perform a Beatles medley at the Brit Awards

MARCH
The band film the Everything Changes video and rehearse for their European tour in Spain

MARCH 16
The European tour starts in Rotterdam. By the end of April, they play 22 concerts in Holland, Belgium, Germany, Switzerland, Austria and Italy

APRIL 9
Everything Changes enters the UK singles chart, going on to become their fourth number 1

MAY 24
Gary Barlow wins an Ivor Novello award for 'Songwriter of the Year' and another for 'Pray'

JUNE
The band fly out to Japan and Australia for promotional trips

July 9
Love Ain't Here Anymore enters the UK singles chart. It peaks at number 3

JULY
The band begins recording a new album

AUGUST 24
The first night of the Pops Tour at Glasgow SECC. The two-month schedule takes in 36 concerts in Glasgow, Manchester, Dublin, Sheffield, Cardiff, London, Birmingham and Belfast

OCTOBER 15
Sure enters the UK singles chart, reaches number 1 and stays on the chart for 15 weeks

NOVEMBER
A promotional trip to Holland and Italy – working with the fashion designer Gianni Versace. The band play at the Concert of Hope in front of Princess Diana – a 50-minute show at Wembley Arena

Robbie Williams's close-cropped hair demonstrated a change of image

Jason takes off: It's all over with Gimme Five Jenny

Monday, November 28, 1994

Pop idol Jason Orange and sexy children's TV presenter Jenny Powell have split up after just three months together.

The Take That heart-throb fell for the curvy, dark-haired TV host after appearing on her Saturday morning show, 'Gimme Five'.

The couple tried to keep their romance secret for fear of upsetting Take That's army of loyal fans but, inevitably, news of their relationship broke out.

Soon after they met the couple were accused of keeping their Manchester neighbours awake with their noisy late-night sex romps.

But now Jason, 24, admits: "Jenny and I are just friends now. We're pals.

"She's a lovely girl but there's no romance between us now. We're not in love.

"It's easier that way. It's not fair for any girl to go out with someone like me.

"I'm just not around long enough for anyone to have a stable relationship with me.

"I only spend a few days at home out of every month and that's no basis for a proper relationship."

TAKE TWO

The popularity of Take That and other bands such as Blur and Oasis prompted children to buy music rather than video games as sales of CDs grew.

Take That... and that and that

Monday, December 5, 1994

Pop heroes Take That covered themselves in glory yesterday.

The Manchester pin-ups scooped top awards in seven categories at the Smash Hits Poll Winners Party, including world's best group and Britain's best group.

Their London rivals East 17 ended up with three booby prizes. They were named worst band, singer Brian Harvey was chosen as least fanciable male and their haircuts were judged worst of the year too.

But East 17 were voted second-best in the world group, British group and album sections.

Still, Take That – with Mark Owen voted most fanciable male – were the undoubted stars of yesterday's televised London party.

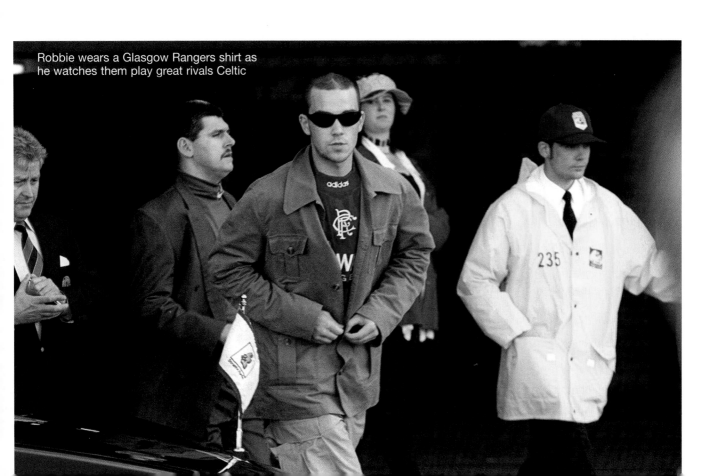

Robbie wears a Glasgow Rangers shirt as he watches them play great rivals Celtic

THEN THERE WAS FOUR

BACK FOR GOOD WAS RELEASED AND BECAME AN INSTANT CLASSIC, SELLING FASTER THAN ANY NON-CHARITY SINGLE IN HISTORY. HOWEVER, CRACKS BEGAN TO APPEAR AND BY JULY FIVE BECAME FOUR AS ROBBIE WILLIAMS QUIT THE GROUP. WAS THE END APPROACHING?

That's a record!
Quick hit outsells Beatles

Tuesday, April 25, 1995

Take That's chart-topper 'Back For Good' earned a place in the record books this week – as Britain's fastest selling non-charity single.

Just over a year ago, the Manchester boys paid tribute to The Beatles with a medley of their hits at the Brit Awards.

Now they have smashed their heroes' record which they set 30 years ago with 'Can't Buy Me Love'.

Remarkably, the band's sixth number one was written by Gary Barlow in just 15 minutes.

"That's a bit long for me," jokes Gary. "But then I did have a coffee break during the writing.

"The songs that I write the quickest seem to come out the best.

"I know some people think that if we put out a record of us burping it would be a huge hit, but that doesn't mean we're going to go down the easy road for easy hits.

"We want to make quality records. We want to better ourselves."

The single has now sold more than 700,000 copies, putting it in the same league as Britain's biggest selling record of all time — Band Aid's 'Do They Know It's Christmas' which eventually notched up sales of 3.5 million.

This has added to Take That's financial success.

They earn £1 million a month – and there seems to be no ceiling on what they can rake in.

Just a few days ago the Manchester heart-throbs signed a lucrative new £20 million deal with their record company and they release their new LP 'Nobody Else' next Monday.

The title track was written by Barlow for his mum and dad, who steered his career in his early days.

He says: "I decided to write a song for them one day when they were looking through old photographs of themselves. I was very touched."

Earlier this week the band announced a string of British shows which will rake in a further £3 million from ticket sales and merchandising.

"It's hard to believe that all this is happening to us, especially as so many people have said we wouldn't last," says Gary.

"They said we were going to split up but that couldn't be further from the truth. Things are just getting better and better."

Take That – featuring Gary, Mark Owen, Jason Orange, Howard Donald and Robbie Williams – hope to double their income by cracking the American pop market.

Their campaign will begin later this year when they frolic half-naked in the California sun as guests on Baywatch.

Not that the TV show's busty star Pamela Anderson has bowled them over. "I'm not really into Pam," says Jason. "I'm not into plastic surgery."

Only Robbie Williams, who has dyed his hair bright red, admits he finds her attractive: "I like Pam, but I like bimbos," he says.

Even so, they've all been working out to make sure their bodies are super-lean for their beach scene.

The once chubby Gary has lost one-and-a-half stones. "One of the things that made me go on a diet was when I saw that chubby, horrible Spitting Image puppet of me on TV," Gary says.

The band's single 'Back For Good' and the forthcoming album show a much more mature side to the group. For their current European tour they also have a more sophisticated image and are dressed by top designers Dolce & Gabbana at an estimated cost of £100,000.

Playing to 250,000 fans and notching up a further £4 million, the band are trying to appeal to a wider audience.

"But we don't want to leave our teenage fans behind," says Mark. "They mean everything to us."

Their female devotees, some as young as 14, show no signs of letting go. They are leaving explicit messages on the band's two tour buses promising nights of passion, and they include their phone numbers.

"The girls will do anything to spend a night with the group," says an insider.

Meanwhile, the boys are looking for yet more challenges. This may mean working separately, hence rumours of a split.

Robbie says: "I can see us taking a break from each other to do various projects but that is way down the line.

"Take That is the main thing and we will be around as long as the fans want us."

Above: Tension rose as Robbie grew apart from the rest of the group

EWLY-blond Robbie salutes ...ctory after sinking a fair few

1995

JANUARY
The band begin recording their new album at Gary's house

FEBRUARY 20
Take That perform Back For Good at the Brits

APRIL 8
Back For Good enters the UK singles chart and is the band's sixth number 1. It becomes the fastest selling non-charity record of all time

Above: The other boys felt that Robbie went off the rails in early 1995. Left, the unhappiness is evident at one of the last public appearances of all five together, at a charity event in June

EXCLUSIVE

Robbie quits Take That

By KATE THORNTON

TAKE That star Robbie Williams has quit the hit band drained by its success.

The 21-year-old singer was said to be "hurt, scared and devastated at the way things have turned out." A source said: "He's exhausted and bored, and can't cope with the group's schedule." Robbie's

● Turn to Page 13

Above and right: How the Mirror reported the news that Robbie Williams had quit Take That

---

Daily Mirror EXCLUSIVE ON NEW

I just need some time to grow up

HE was always the one who made the fans laugh. But lately Robbie had stopped laughing himself.

The endless tours and sleepless nights had taken their toll on the 21-year-old who has known nothing but stardom since he left school at 16.

By KATE THORNTON

I noticed something amiss with Robbie back in March when I found him in a bar in Munich — sober, both in mind and attitude.

"What you don't understand is I've never had a chance grow up and be an adolescer he said when I asked him explain the long face.

"I came from school strai into this. The others have had a couple of years to f their feet and do the thi teenage blokes do.

"Now if I fall down dru and make a fool of mys the pictures are on t front pages the next d

"I'm not the wild on Take That — I'm just youngest."

In one sentence Rok summed up exactly he was unable to c with being Rob Williams.

Serious

Like the other memt of the band he's had training, but the adv tage they had on him experience of real life

He'd never drawr wage packet, never ha serious girlfriend a never had the chance be young at heart.

The peroxide blond v always the loude smartest and mc attention-grabbing. to the few who got cl to Robbie it was a dif ent story.

Beneath the showm was a boy lacking in c fidence, bursting w talent and in desper need of someone to l him.

Pillow

Never one to sleep night, he would rub herbal sleeping reme that his mum alwa packed in his case on hotel pillow.

Then, notepad in ha Robbie would spend ho writing poetry.

Then hours agonis over who in his ev expanding entourage

GOING IT ALONE: Take That will survive, but Robbie will be missed

OFFICIAL New Take That

THAT STUNNED THE POP WORLD

Robbie quits

● From Page One

stunning departure comes at the height of the five-piece band's success – and just three weeks before their £2million sell-out UK tour.

Last night, Take That's Mark Owen said the rest of the group were so shocked by Robbie's decision they had thought of splitting up.

But he said they would carry on, and declared: "We love what we do much we couldn't possibly call it a day."

Choreographer Jason Orange said: "We'll all miss Robbie. But we feel the only way to go now is forward."

Robbie's decision to leave the band, made after weeks of soul-searching, means giving up millions of pounds in future earnings.

Actor

It is believed he will now take time off before launching a solo career as an actor or singer.

Scotching rumours that the heart-throb had been fired by manager Nigel Martin-Smith, band member Gary Barlow said: "Why on earth sack him weeks before a UK tour?

"We wanted him to stay at least for that. But he has left the group of his own accord."

Martin-Smith said: "Robbie feels he is no longer able to give Take That the long-term commitment they need."

Teen idols Take That – known as the Fab Five – have had a succession of hits since bursting on the scene in 1992.

A friend of Robbie's family said in the star's home city of Stoke-on-Trent last night: "This has come like a bolt from the blue."

Fax YOUR message to the band

MILLIONS of fans will be heartbroken to see Robbie go. You can send him a farewell message – or even a desperate plea to stay. Just fax this number.

0171 293 3409

NOW FOR SOME REAL LIFE: I'm not the wildest member of the band, just the youngest, says 21-year-old Robbie

...ould read it to without ...eeling embarrassed.

"I'm quite a shy ...loke," he told me ...nce. "I'm a sensitive ...oul and I love my ...num."

His way of dealing ...vith the intense pres-...ure that came with is ...is fame was to get ...drunk, be outrageous ...nd pull stupid faces ...vhen the cameras ...came out.

Surrender

Robbie refused to ...become a prisoner to ...is fame. Rather than ...urrender to it he tried ...o have fun with it.

Last month, amid ...rumours that he was ...itting the bottle, he ...appeared on MTV wear-...ng a T-shirt with the slogan "My Booze Hell".

"My mum will love this," he said.

Five minutes later — live on air — he accept-ed a bet to flash his rear for £10. And with the cash in his hand dropped his trousers for an estimated 60 mil-lion European viewers.

Despite his woman-iser reputation, he has never had a serious girlfriend.

He was linked to a string of celebrities and attractive models but a long-term commit-ment was something he could only look for-ward to.

Like the rest of the band he had to avoid a serious relationship - not because of his fans,

but because he couldn't afford to get hurt.

"We're never home. It would be a nightmare going with one of us, and we can't afford to get attached," he said with a hint of regret.

His departure from Take That will mean a departure of Robbie's huge fan base.

Popular

Outside of Britain, he was the most popu-lar member of the group. While on tour, undying declarations of love for him out-numbered those for Mark, Gary, Howard and Jason.

Without him, Take That have weakened what is the strongest unit in the pop world.

Second to Gary Barlow, Robbie is the group's finest vocalist.

He missed out on singing lead vocals on their latest album, Nobody Else, because he lost his voice.

"I just wasn't good enough to carry a lead vocal. It's that sim-ple," he told me in April.

"I abused my voice and missing out on singing on the album was the kick up the arse I needed. I was going out too much at night and I paid the price."

His lead vocals can be carried by Gary, Howard or Mark when the group open their tour on August 5 in Manchester — but he will be sorely missed.

Robbie's army of teenage fans will cry for him, some may even shun the concerts out of loyalty to him.

But Take That will go on. They've broken every record in the book, outsold the Bea-tles and wormed their way into the hearts of millions with their in-fectious songs and per-sonalities.

Craggy

It won't be the same without Rob. In a bland cosmos of music dom-inated with faceless artists and craggy pop cardigans, he was re-freshing.

I dare anyone who has ever met him not to like him.

MAY 13
Nobody Else enters the album chart, reaches number 1 and stays on the chart for 33 weeks

JUNE 1
The band appear on MTV's Most Wanted

JUNE
Robbie Williams goes to Glastonbury and joins Oasis on stage

JULY 15
The band fly to London minus Robbie Williams. For the next two weeks they rehearse in London

JULY 17
Robbie Williams announces that he's leaving Take That

AUGUST 5
Never Forget enters the UK singles chart. It reaches number 1 and stays on the chart for 9 weeks. The band start their Nobody Else Tour at the new Manchester Arena. They play 10 gigs in Manchester and 10 at Earls Court

AUGUST 12
Back For Good enters the American Hot 100. It makes number 7

AUGUST 26
Nobody Else (US version) enters the album chart. It reaches number 26

SEPTEMBER 25
The band start their Australian/Asian tour at the Adelaide Entertainment Centre. They also play Melbourne Flinders Park, Sydney Entertainment Centre, Brisbane Entertainment Centre, Perth Entertainment Centre, Bangkok Hua Mark Indoor Stadium, Singapore Indoor Stadium, Tokyo Yoyogi Olympic Stadium and the Djkarta Istorn Senayan

DECEMBER
Take That pick up several awards at the Smash Hits Poll Winners Party and perform Back For Good and Never Forget

THAT'S

Mega band could fold next year

By RICHARD WALLACE and KATE THORNTON

TEEN idols Take That – Britain's mos successful ever band – could break up by next year, insiders predicted last night

Songwriter Gary Barlow is believed to be thinking of leaving. Fellow Fab Five Robbie Williams, exhausted and disillusioned by fame, has already announced his shock departure.

SOLO HOPES: Star Gary

A senior executive with the group's record company, RCA, declared "I'd be surprised if Take That were still together in 1996.

"Gary has a huge talent and a solo career is the obvious move.

"Robbie's departure is only the tip of the iceberg.

"They all feel slightly constrained by being Take That."

Love

Yesterday, anguished fans begged 21-year-old Robbie to stay in a series of heart-rending messages spelling out their loss.

As they did so, Take That's remaining members — Gary and Jason Orange, both 24, Mark Owen, 23, and Howard Donald, 27 — told of their sadness at Robbie's departure...and vowed to carry on.

Confirming there were no plans to replace their pal, Gary said: "You couldn't — there's no other Rob and if we searched the world we'd struggle to find one.

"If he has a change of heart, the door's still open and we'll be waiting.

"But the rest of us still love the business so much — we're not ready to go yet.

Speaking in a radio interview from their hotel in London's Hyde Park, Gary and Mark disclosed that Robbie broke the news that he wanted to quit two weeks ago.

Mark, who said the band's first thought was to split, said: "He left last Thursday and we gave him the weekend to think about it.

"When he came back, he hadn't changed his mind.

"Since then, we've been trying to carry on. But it was quite obvious to us he wasn't happy.

"We had an agreement to give six months notice if anyone wanted to leave.

"But we decided that we didn't want to put a mate through that pain and thought he should go."

Even though Robbie's decision came on the eve of the band's UK tour next month, the boys denied they felt let down.

TAKE FAX

DEVASTATED Take That fans bombarded the Mirror with faxes yesterday.

Most wrote begging Robbie Williams to stay, but some were critical, accusing the singer of being a "deserter".

Here are some of the messages that were sent:

If you have to leave, leave after the tour. Think of this as a farewell tour — something for all the fans to remember you by — Love Melanie Ball, Blackpool, Lancs.

Robbie, so young when fame came. No chance to play a young man's game. So passionate in all that you do. "Capture the moment", that describes you – Sue McDonald, Southend, Essex.

I will miss you a lot. You have always been my best member of Take That — Roni E. Ingram, aged nine, Ilford, Essex.

Robbie, although "Everything Changes", I'm "Sure" it "Could be Magic" and you can "Relight My Fire" anytime "Babe". I just "Pray" that you will stay with "Take That and Party" "Forever" – Love Fiona, Karen and Joanne, Leeds.

Don't go Robbie we love you. "It Only Takes a Minute" to change your mind — Love and kisses from Shaz, Kate, Wen and Simone (your biggest fans ever).

Dear Take That and Robbie, Please don't leave us – but if that is what you want to do we will support you all the way. But we will never stop loving Take That – from Laura H and Laura P.

Robbie, I am very sad that you are leaving Take That. You always made me laugh when I was feeling down. Please change your mind but if you don't, good luck with your

solo career — *My endless love, Selina, Dublin.*

Robbie is our hero, you've made us so blue. We just can't believe the bad vibes are true.

We wish you luck Robbie, in everything you do. We'll miss you so much babe. You won't believe it's true. We love you – Sal and Sue, Huddersfield.

To Robbie, Please don't go you deserter. Or we won't love you any more — Love Kerry, Felecia and Suzy.

Robbie, My love for you will never tire. So come on Robbie, Relight My Fire! Please don't go!! – N. Butler, Harold Wood, Essex.

Rob, How could you deprive the female population of the sexiest body on earth, not to mention the funniest, most entertaining guy around? I am totally heartbroken. Life will never be the same again. I love you — Anna, aged 21, Oldham, Lancs.

My darling Robbie, Don't do it! Remember what happened to Andrew Ridgeley — Sarah Pollard, London.

Rob, I can't say I'm not shocked because I am. But don't worry, I don't think you have let anyone down. I am only a couple of weeks older than you and I realise you must have missed out on a lot of "normal" life. I wish you all the luck for your future — Love R Whitelegg, Altrincham, Cheshire.

My darling Rob, If this page seems damp, then it's because it's splattered with my tears – tears that I can't stop from falling. I've cried so hard I've now got a headache, but I don't care. All my love forever – Suzanne McIlquam, aged 26, Worsley, Manchester.

GO, GO, GO!
(AND TAKE THE REST WITH YOU)

Right: More reaction to the Robbie departure – and what proved an accurate prediction that the end could be approaching for the group

END OF THAT!

HELP ME I'VE GONE

EXCLUSIVE *Daily Mirror* OFFER

HERE'S Robbie with the rest of Take That in the group's 1996 official calendar which goes on sale next month. Hailed as The Last Official Calendar, demand will be massive. But we're giving fans a chance to buy this memento before it hits the shops. It's a fantastic, exclusive Daily Mirror offer. And tomorrow we'll be giving you details of how you can get what will soon be a treasure for all Take That fans.

OH BOY! Robbie as a cheeky kid — now he wants to spread his wings

Robbie didn't tell me, says dad

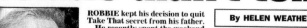

SURPRISED: Dad Peter

1: "I don't feel r towards him. ot been happy. have carried on ed the money. old us all about ack to him." ring a break in at the London e band comfort- fans outside. said: "We want to know we d a row. Robbie dn't take any sure. want you to for all of us. 't know where you lot find him, him all at one. sh him."

By HELEN WEATHERS

ROBBIE kept his decision to quit Take That secret from his father.

He recently spent the weekend with ex-copper Peter Conway, but gave no hint that he was thinking of going solo.

And he had said he was looking forward to the group's forth-coming UK tour.

Peter revealed last night: "The first thing I knew about it was when a fan phoned me up in tears and said, 'Tell me it's not true.'

"This has come as a complete surprise. When I saw Robbie a couple of weeks ago, he was talk-ing about the tour and how he was going to be very busy for the next few months because of it.

"He didn't say anything about leaving the band. The only thing he did say was that he was very tired."

Peter, 50, who split from Robbie's mother in 1977, said his son often travelled to Stoke-on-Trent, Staffs, to see him.

"When he's home, he doesn't talk about the band at all, unless someone asks him," he said. "He just wants to relax, go down the pub for a pint with his old mates, and play football for the local team."

Peter, an entertainments man-ager for a Cheshire hotel, added: "I've tried to speak to him today but his phone is off the hook and he has gone to ground.

"If he is planning a solo career, he would have thought long and hard about it. He is not the type to rush into anything.

"I thought he was coping well with the pressures, but none of us envisaged just how big Take That were going to be. Robbie was with me at a holiday camp when he got the phone call to say that he was in the band. He was delighted.

"But I never thought my son would end up a superstar adored by millions of girls. At the end of the day, though, I just think of him as my son.

"The first thing I'll say to him when I see him is, 'Fancy a pint'?"

And if the solo career doesn't work out as Robbie hopes, he can always work for his dad.

"I'm holding auditions now for new acts — I would love him to turn up," added Peter.

The show must go on: Gary, Mark,
Howard and Jason at the 1995
Smash Hits Poll Winners Party

42

Take the lot

Monday, December 4, 1995

Take That. And that. And that. And this. And that. The teen idols swept the board at last night's Smash Hits awards.

There was no holding them.

Not only was the band voted Best Group, the magazine's teenage readers, somewhat confusingly, also voted them Britain's Worst Group.

But if there had been a category for Best Group In The Whole Universe Since The Beginning Of Time the lads would have walked away with it.

Mark Owen was Most Fanciable Male and Best Dressed Person, despite turning out for the presentations at the London Arena in a gold lame dress.

And since this was an all-Take That night, dreadlocked Howard Donald picked up the Tragic Haircut award. Even Robbie Williams, who walked out on the band, wasn't left out.

The group's teeny-fans voted him Sad Loser Of The Year.

Take That have now equalled the record set by Duran Duran who won the Best Group title four times between 1982-1985.

"This has been a fantastic way to end the year," Mark Owen said. "I'm thinking of putting up a new shelf for my awards when I get home."

New shelf? More like a new living room…

TAKE TWO

Robbie Williams was said to be planning to record a Christmas single with Louise Nurding, who had left Eternal within 24 hours of Robbie quitting Take That.

44

On stage for the first time since Robbie left, at the new Manchester Arena in August

Above: The costumes became more elaborate as the years went by. The top picture shows a triumphant performance at the Smash Hits Poll Winners Party, where they picked up 10 awards

GOODBYE...FOR NOW

AFTER AN INCREDIBLE FIVE YEARS, TAKE THAT FORMALLY SPLIT IN FEBRUARY, GOING OUT AT THE TOP BEFORE EMBARKING ON THEIR SOLO CAREERS. GARY BARLOW FOUND HAPPINESS IN HIS PRIVATE LIFE BUT BITTERNESS LINGERED FROM ROBBIE'S DEPARTURE A YEAR EARLIER

Were they THAT good?
By Mike Stock – the producer
who turned them down

Wednesday, February 14, 1996

When Take That burst into the charts, I could have kicked myself.

This was the band I had been offered and turned down.

There have been times over the last five years when I have sorely regretted that decision, but that's hindsight for you.

Now it's easy to see why these five young lads became one of Britain's most successful pop groups, and I am saddened they are now splitting up.

While other bands had one or two of the right ingredients for stardom, Take That had all of them. They were like a jigsaw possessing all the pieces which fitted together perfectly.

But when they first turned up to meet me I wasn't interested. I can't even remember the impression they made on me. We were busy with our own stable of young stars, Kylie Minogue and Jason Donovan, and felt we had enough all-boy bands with Brother Beyond, Big Fun and Dead or Alive.

In the early days Take That's records were not very good, and I didn't lose any sleep over not producing them. That was to change.

Today the news of their split will affect their fans in the same way the news of the Beatles splitting affected me a quarter of a century ago.

Each generation has its own supergroup and I believe Take That will go down in history as one of the great pop bands of the 1990s. But only time will tell if they will be regarded in 20 years' time as another Beatles or Bay City Rollers.

On the face of it the Beatles and Take That have nothing in common. The Beatles started off by writing and performing their own songs, while Take That began with other people's songs.

The Beatles conquered America while Take That, much to their regret, never quite did. The Beatles were at the top for eight years before splitting up in 1970. Take That managed six.

Paul McCartney and John Lennon's songs still sound as good as they did 30 years ago. We've yet to see if Gary Barlow's songs stand the test of time.

Like the Beatles, Take That had that 'X Factor' – that certain chemistry. They came up with a unique blend of lively dance pop and stuck with it, always giving their fans what they wanted. But all good things have to come to an end and they are quitting at the top.

1996

FEBRUARY 6
The band perform How Deep Is Your Love on the Des O'Connor Show

FEBRUARY 12
Rumours start to circle that Take That is to split up

FEBRUARY 13
The band confirm the split at their last press conference held in Manchester Airport Hilton

MARCH 9
How Deep Is Your Love enters the UK singles chart and reaches number 1

MARCH 29
The Daily Mirror breaks the news of Gary Barlow's relationship with Dawn Andrews

APRIL 5
Take That make their last public appearance, in Holland, where they perform Back For Good and How Deep Is Your Love

APRIL 6
A compilation album Greatest Hits enters the chart at number 1

JULY 20
Gary Barlow's first solo record Forever Love enters the UK singles charts and makes the number 1 spot

AUGUST
Robbie Williams's solo debut Freedom reaches number 2 in the charts

NOVEMBER
Mark Owen's first solo record Child peaks at number 3 in the charts

47

Left and above: The Daily Mirror reacts to the Take That split. On the opposite page, the boys wave goodbye at the press conference where they confirmed the news

THAT'S THAT

TAKE OF

'Our dream is t return and do it all over again

By MATTHEW WRIGHT
DIARY SPECIAL

SPLITTING pop idols Take That are already planning a comeback – in the 21st century.

Band leader Gary Barlow revealed hopes of a reunion when the break-up was confirmed yesterday.

First came the bad news for fans — that the four favourites were going their separate ways. "It's something we've been thinking about for the last six months," said Gary, 25. "It's a career move for each of us."

Then his good news: "But our dream is to return and do it all over again after five or 10 years."

Take That's decision to bow out was announced on the 22nd birthday of sacked group member Robbie Williams.

Last night he said: "I find it difficult to respond. It's my birthday and I'm off to celebrate. Frankly, I'm more concerned about how Port Vale do in the Cup. I did my grieving when I was kicked out of the band last June."

I was at a hastily-arranged press conference at Manchester's Hilton Hotel when Gary said: "The rumours are true.

"How Deep Is Your Love will be our last single and the Greatest Hits will be our last album."

Take That first got together nearly six years ago. Since then the band has scored seven No 1 chart hits, four of them consecutively.

Awards

Strangely, they decided to break up just weeks after their first American top ten hit Back For Good, which reached No 7.

Their final British performance will be at the Brit Award ceremony on Monday night. It will be screened on ITV the following evening.

But the band still have some European engagements.

Their final gig will not take place until April 5 when they appear on a Dutch TV show.

The four band members, all millionaires, say the decision to split was finally taken last month.

Heart-throb Mark Owen, 24, said "We had a meeting and all went in with the same thing on our minds."

He added: "The time is right. We took it all to a level beyond our expectations."

The band said nothing about their feelings for Robbie, sacked last July

Solo

When Gary was reminded that it was Robbie's birthday he replied drily "Is it?"

He admitted that the band had planned to announce their split at the Brit Awards but changed their minds as rumours about the break up grew

Gary also used the press conference to announce details of his solo career

"I've not had that much time to think about it," he said "But as usual I've got lots of material

"Hopefully I'll have my first single out by the summer followed closely by the album and do some concerts this year"

The rest of Take That assured the press they had various musical projects in the pipeline but refused to go into details

Howard Donald 27 laughed off suggestions that he would become a drummer

And Mark turned on a Radio 1 reporter who insisted on asking Gary about his solo career

"What about my solo career," said Mark

"First I'm getting a job on Radio 1 your job"

Howard chipped in "I thought you were going to do a photo set for Play boy"

But Mark continued

Actually I asked my mum to get me a job at a bakery."

When Jason Orange was asked about his plans for the future he said "I'm going to buy a goat"

But as his band mates giggled, an embarrassed looking Jason explained he preferred drinking

OLD BOYS: We show how the lads might look by the time their 2006 get-together comes arc

Odds on a solo hit

BOOKIES yesterday laid odds on the boys' chances of solo success.

Singer Gary Barlow is hot favourite at 6/4 on to hit the No.1 spot first. Ladbrokes quoted Robbie Williams at 2/1 and Mark Owen at 6/1, with Jason Orange and Howard Donald at 50/1. The group has also been tipped for Best Single at the Brit awards.

Hear their farewe

YOU can hear Take That's farewell to their by calling our special hotline. Ring 0891 252 to listen to the boys announcing their split at a conference.

Calls cost 39p per minute cheap rate and 49p per minute other times. Lines close at midnight on Wednesday, Februa

CALL NOW 0891 252 64

goats' milk for health reasons

Singer and dancer Jason, 25, disclosed that the group decided against following the example of Wham and doing a massive goodbye concert.

News of the break-up devastated the band's die-hard fans who

gathered outside the conference.

One said: "In th concert Howard pr they would stay to as long as the wanted them to.

"We don't want th break up, however, concert would be n

But Jason insiste talked about a farewe to say goodbye to o but decided not to.

"It's not worth back for another money."

GARY SPLITS GROUP

● From Page One

stormed the charts, they have notched up seven No 1s and massive record sales worldwide.

Their success has meant a whacking £6.5m for Gary, who earned more through songwriting royalties. The others have made do with £1.5m each. Speculation had been

mounting that Britain's most successful group since the Beatles were about to split.

The Mirror revealed last summer how Gary wanted a solo career

Yesterday he finally confirmed the fans' worst fears. "The rumours are true," he said at a press conference.

Last night Samaritans

were manning phone lines to deal with calls from heartbroken fans.

The split stunned bosses at record company RCA, which has made an estimated £80m from the band.

They stood to make even more with Take That poised to conquer the lucrative US market. One executive said: "It's frustrating, but with Gary at

least we've got a chance to launch him in America on the back of Take That."

Gary yesterday called the decision a "career move" for the whole band.

Heart-throb Mark said at the chaotic press conference: "We do care very much about our fans."

But one heartbroken teenager said: "Gary instigated this. They are letting us down."

BUT DON'T F YOU MUSIC F

THE world's oldest has recorded a CD and techno music.

Proceeds will hel year-old Jeanne Ca buy a mini-bus fo nursing home wher lives in southern Fr

Producer Philippe mas said: "She real into this project."

WERE THEY THAT GOOD – PAGE 6

FOR 10 YEARS

AT'S ALL, FOLKS: Farewell – for now – from the band at their press conference yesterday　Picture ANDREW STENNING

SMART START: Boys in the early days

Samaritans on standby

THE Samaritans, Take That, their record label and German state authorities set up special phone lines last night to help distraught fans.

Their fears were highlighted by the attempted suicide of a teenager in Berlin when Robbie Williams left. The Samar-

itans' number, 0345 90 90, will be displayed in lights at London's Piccadilly Circus throughout the day.

HEART THROBS: Young fans fell in love

Sad day for record firm

RCA issued an official statement confirming the group's split.

The record company, which filmed yesterday's press conference for possible video release, said: "This is a very sad day but we are all extremely positive about the future."

Paying tribute to the

group's phenomenal success RCA said: "We look forward to hearing about their plans."

MEGASTARS: By 1994 they were huge

No fake, we must break

MIMIC band Fake That copied their heroes to the last yesterday – and called it a day.

The Isle of Wight-based lookalikes have always been genuinely consistent.

When Robbie Williams quit Take That last year, they axed their "Robbie." Last night singer Freddy

Lee, 23, sighed: "Now it makes sense for us to quit, too."

He plans to ape Gary Barlow and go solo.

49

Above: The end – but Gary says they hope to return in 10 years and "do it all over again". While that prediction was spot on, the Mirror's unflattering suggestion of how they might look in 2006 proved less accurate

THAT'S ME FREE!

'It was like six years in prison .. I've been confused, betrayed and sad' – ROBBIE WILLIAMS

ROCK AROUND THE DOCK: Robbie has given up fighting his record company   Picture: TOM HOWARD

That's me free!

Tuesday, February 27, 1996

Former Take That star Robbie Williams has told for the first time how working with the band was a hateful six-year 'prison' sentence.

He sensationally claimed the idols lived a public lie, always under orders how to behave. "Take That as you know them didn't exist," he said.

And he revealed that since quitting he had felt "confused, betrayed, angry, sad and disappointed" – and had tried to drown his sorrows in drink.

Robbie poured out his heart days before going to the High Court in a bid to quit his contract with record company BMG.

But yesterday, threatened by bankruptcy, the 22-year-old star gave up on his fight. An out-of-court settlement left him still tied to the company – and facing a bill of at least £500,000.

"I'm extremely sorry I ever brought the case," he said.

Earlier, speaking to Smash Hits magazine, Robbie said of his time with the group: "It was a prison and I lived in that prison for six years."

In a dig at the band's manager, Nigel Martin-Smith, he said: "I was never allowed an opinion. We were told what to say, how to behave, how to dress and where we could and couldn't go. All of the thinking was done for us.

"I hate to shatter the myth, but Take That as you know them don't exist. Instead, the group aren't too dissimilar from the Loch Ness monster – they live beneath the surface and never show who they really are."

Robbie quit the band in July hoping to launch his own solo career. The group has now split up.

But freedom only brought bitter anguish. Robbie says in the magazine: "It was like I'd been protected from the world, then suddenly someone threw me from a 200ft building, saying 'See how you get on when you land!'

"I was betrayed by them. I know I sound bitter, but I am bitter. The past six months have been an emotional rollercoaster. I've been isolated."

To ease the pain, Robbie hit the bottle. He said: "I got drunk and fell over a lot. It wasn't an answer to my problems. It added to them.

"Not having anything to do was the hardest thing. I let myself waste away. Now I know the party's over."

Robbie has only spoken twice to Take That since the split – both times at awards ceremonies. But he still pines for his best mate, band member Mark Owen, 24.

He said: "I worry about Mark because I love him. I don't care about the others at all.

"Mark was my confidante and my buddy. I'd love to see him now more than anything. Just me and him in a room to talk. There isn't a day when I don't think about him. But I'm scared that if I see him again he'll be the same person he was when I left.

"I don't think I could cope with that – with him being Mark the myth, not the real Mark.

"Just talking about it chokes me. When I think about him it makes me cry. But if I'm honest I lost Mark before I left Take That, and he lost me.

"We wanted different things. I wanted to be heard and he, like the others, didn't listen."

Robbie was speaking when he was desperate to leave BMG. He said of his forthcoming court case: "I can't even think about losing. I wouldn't be doing myself justice if I didn't fight for what's mine.

"I haven't got the money people think I have. If I lose, it will leave me bankrupt; you've got to stand up for yourself." Yesterday, that fight was over.

Under an eleventh-hour deal, Robbie stays tied to BMG – owners of Take That's ROA label – but is expected to switch to the Deconstruction label.

He has surrendered his right to veto the group's Greatest Hits LP, which will now come out later next month.

He is also believed to have paid his legal team about £500,000 and must strike a deal with BMG for costs.

BMG said: "We're delighted Robbie has accepted the validity of our contract. It's a shame he didn't talk to us before the start of all this."

Left and below:
Howard and
Jason leaving a
party for the
group in
Manchester in
January

Right: The Mirror's
exclusive pictures
from Take That's
final video, 'How
Deep Is Your Love?'

Take That bow out with No.1

Monday, March 4, 1996

Take That last night shot to the top of the British charts with their farewell single.

The pop group took over the top spot from rivals Oasis with their version of the 1978 Bee Gees classic 'How Deep Is Your Love', which was released last Monday.

It is the Manchester band's eighth No. 1 hit.

With Oasis currently grabbing the spotlight after picking up three Brit Awards, Take That's success proves they still have massive backing.

Fans were distraught last month when the group announced they were to split. But the success of the single means their greatest hits compilation now looks almost certain to dominate the album charts.

Its release on March 26 follows a court battle with former member Robbie Williams, who threatened to veto it.

Matthew Wri[ght]

SHOW

CLIFF HANGER: All smiles now, but it's the end of the line for C

BAND'S ALL A BLUR

I'M deeply concerned for the future of the Blur boys after half the band failed to turn up for an important gig.

It's the second time this month group members have been missing from shows.

Guitarist Graham Coxon was replaced by a cardboard cut-out at Italy's San Remo pop festival on Tuesday night. And a roadie had to fill in for bass player Alex James

after he went AWOL. Only singer Damon and drummer Dave Rowntree bothered to turn up for punters — some of whom had paid up to £600 a ticket.

But worried tour manager Ivan Thomas told me: "The band isn't going to split...they could operate as a three-piece or a two piece — even a one piece if things start getting really bad."

WRIGH[T]

"DON'T B
by this b
They wil
rape and
our wo
invade A
Hole's
singer C

'S DIARY EXCLUSIVE

E OFF GARY

GET KNOTTED: Gary, Mark, Jason and Howard face a grisly end as they perch on the edge of a reservoir

Take That's final video

THESE are the last moments of Gary Barlow, a cold and miserable end for the star of Take That.

The band is winding down its affairs — and in its final video Gary is killed off, sent to a watery grave by model Paula Hamilton.

Tied to a chair, perched precariously on the bank of a reservoir Gary pleads for his life to the strains of the band's new single, *How Deep Is Your Love?*, a cover of the Bee Gees' 1978 hit.

The video is a real tear-jerker, four minutes of heart-stopping drama guaranteed not to leave a dry eye in the house.

It could have been worse. At one stage the script called for all four band members to die — but the idea was considered too distressing for their fans.

Take That ordered five different endings to be made while they debated whether or not to split.

The final choice was only made last Tuesday when they confirmed they were calling it a day — and Gary drew the short straw.

So while Mark, Howard and Jason are merely tied up, tortured and tormented by the girl from the Volkswagen ads Gary gets the worst of it. The idol of a million teenagers disappears over the edge.

And, er, that's That.

FORK-ET ME NOT: Gary gets it from Paula

ture: PHILIP OLLERENSHAW/IDOLS

AMUSED: Mack Cocker

Good on yer, old Cocker

DAD'S JOY OVER BRITS BAD LAD

JARVIS Cocker's Brit Awards outrage might have upset Michael Jackson — but it went down a storm with the dad he hasn't seen for 19 years.

The Pulp singer has taken legal advice and is demanding an apology from Jacko.

But Mack Cocker chuckled when he heard how his son tried to moon at Jacko. "Good on ya, son," he laughed. "You've got to be the bravest person in the world to wiggle your arse when Michael Jackson's in the proximity."

I tracked down Mack, 64, at his home in Darwin, Australia, yesterday. The former DJ, who walked out when Jarvis

ROW: Yesterday's *Mirror*

was seven, is now keen for a reunion: "It would be great to see him. He's gone up in my estimation after this," he said.

Even Paul Weller's mum Ann called me to defend Jarvis, who was arrested on suspicion of assault. "Jarvis didn't touch those kids. He's a lovely bloke," she said.

As for Jarvis, he told 5,000 fans at a Pulp concert in Brighton: "I don't like people saying I would hit young children or throw them off stage."

Last night Jarvis's spokesman said: "Jackson's statement contained allegations that Jarvis attacked those children but we have evidence that he didn't."

● Justice for Jarvis, page 28

SERIOUS: Jarvis Cocker

Poppet on a String

ETER Stringfellow was on acking form the other ght when he hosted the ats of the Miss GB/Universe beauty competition.

After roping me in to be e of the sharp-eyed judges, ter, 55, got the evening ing at his exclusive London ub with a string of near-the uckle gags.

He'll never forgive me for repeating this one, but I raised an eyebrow when he quipped: "I've interfered with more teenagers than anyone else in London."

Thankfully, Peter's 16-year-old girlfriend Helen Benoist has many fabulous assets including a huge sense of humour.

I only hope her parents feel the same way....

WRIGHT LINES

"MY father once told me I should develop my body because I wasn't born with much brain and it was the only thing I had to fall back on."

Sylvester Stallone

HITCH FOR HUGH

IS IT possible that Liz Hurley and Hugh Grant are secretly engaged?

My spies in France tell me Liz has referred to Hugh as her "fiance" in an interview with *Paris Match* magazine.

The remark has caused hysteria in movie circles, where many still gossip about Hugh's trip down Sunset Boulevard last year. But Karen Smith, at Liz's film company Simian, assures me: "There is nothing in it. Hugh's not her fiance. That's their bad translation."

Hugh's *Restoration* co-star Robert Downey Jnr offered a more amusing explanation: "He and I have been lovers since the early Seventies.

"It's going to take a little bit of adjustment for everyone else, but we're getting a flat together in Mayfair."

Shut up Robbie – Mark hits back at his old mate

Tuesday, March 19, 1996

They used to be best mates, but not any more...Robbie Williams has been told to shut his mouth by Take That's Mark Owen.

Robbie infuriated Mark with a stream of digs at the band and manager Nigel Martin-Smith.

Now Mark, 24, has hit back, warning Robble to stop slagging off the group that made him a millionaire.

And he has criticised the party-loving star for wasting his talent in the eight months since he left the band.

"I'm disappointed in Robbie," says Mark. "He's saying things about us which he's got no right, no reason to be saying.

"He's attacked the lads and by attacking the lads he's attacking me."

It's a remarkable outburst by soft-spoken Mark, considering how close the two pals once were.

Last month Robbie, 22, said: "I'm not that bothered about what happens to the rest of Take That.

"I just hope Mark is okay. He's my friend and we're extremely close."

Not any more, it seems.

"It's sad," Mark tells Denmark's Mix magazine. "It's a shame it ended up like this. I just want Rob to sort himself out.

"I do miss him. For two years we shared rooms. But now I feel sorry for him. I feel like he's been really badly advised."

But Robbie has not completely burned his bridges with his old mate.

Mark admits that if he saw the loudmouth star again, he would probably still say hello.

"I'd put my arm around him and give him a kiss because I believe in forgiveness," he says.

Above: Robbie Williams presenting an award at the Brits in February, days after his former colleagues announced they were disbanding

Take That bow out at the Brits, picking up the Best Single award for 'Back For Good'

56

Matthew Wright's DIARY EXCLUSIVE

GARY'S DANCING QUEEN!

RAUNCHY Gary and Dawn, circled, are in perfect harmony on Take That's last-ever tour

DEEP IN LOVE: Gary and Dawn stroll happily hand in hand Picture: ADRIAN TURNER/PAPPIX

THIS is the picture that will break the hearts of Take That fans around the world – the first-ever photo of Gary Barlow with a girlfriend.

The millionaire star — now working on a solo career — has been secretly dating raunchy dancer Dawn Andrews, 23, for seven months.

Gary, 25, fell for the stunning blonde when she appeared on the band's last-ever tour.

Model

Take That manager Nigel Martin Smith had banned the group from having girlfriends in case it damaged their teen heart-throb image.

But part-time model Dawn's revealing outfits and curvy figure were definitely a big hit with Gary.

He became so smitten with her that he even swapped hotels during the 20-date tour last August so they could spend more time together.

The couple, both dressed in scruffy casual clothes, were spotted by the Mirror strolling hand-in-hand on a shopping trip in Chelsea, London. They even sported identical Adidas training shoes as they peered through the windows of expensive designer boutiques.

One shopper said: "They looked truly in love and kept squeezing hands.

"Gary did his best to look anonymous by wearing sunglasses but the couple still drew plenty of stares from passers-by."

Dawn has also spent regular weekends at Gary's £1million mansion hidden away in the Cheshire countryside.

And the star, whose last single with Take That was How Deep Is Your Love, showed his affection for the dancer by introducing her to his mum and dad.

She chatted and joked with Marjorie and Colin during a civic reception for the band in Manchester last month.

● TAKE That's Greatest Hits album, which has already sold an incredible 500,000 copies, is set to shoot straight to Number 1 in the album charts on Sunday.

Beatles soar to top in US

THE Beatles' new album has gone straight in at No.1 in the US charts despite a Radio 1-style airplay ban.

Anthology 2 sold nearly 500,000 copies in a week even though latest single Real Love is blacklisted.

"So-called governors of music taste have got it wrong," said a band source.

CHANGE: Singer Phil

PHIL COLLINS QUITS GENESIS

ROCK superstar Phil Collins is quitting Genesis after more than 20 years with the band.

His departure leaves the group looking for a new singer to finish their 18th album in time for the summer.

Multi-millionaire lead vocalist and drummer Phil, 45, yesterday confirmed he was leaving to concentrate on his

By MATTHEW WRIGHT

solo career. "I felt it was time to change direction," he said.

"I will be doing music for movies, some jazz projects and, of course, my solo career.

"I wish the guys the very best. We remain best friends."

Phil has not recorded an

album with Genesis pals Mike Rutherford and Tony Banks since We Can't Dance in 1991.

The band have sold more than 80 million albums since he took over in 1975 from original vocalist Peter Gabriel.

Insiders claim Phil quit because he could not face the strain of another world tour.

Last night guitarist Mike, 46,

currently touring with his other band Mike And The Mechanics, said: "I understand Phil's reasons for leaving.

"Being in two highly successful outfits is hard work."

After splitting with wife Jill two years ago, Phil now lives in Switzerland with 23-year-old heiress girlfriend Orianne Cevey.

Above: The Mirror reveals that Gary is in a relationship with Take That dancer Dawn Andrews, who he went on to marry in 2000

DAILY Mirror

Friday, April 5, 1996   HONESTY, QUALITY, EXCELLENCE   February daily sale: 3,348,935 *(INCORPORATING THE DAILY RECORD)*   30p

Get the Jackal

EXCLUSIVE By TED OLIVER

IRA sniper stalks VIPs

POLICE have launched a huge operation to prevent an Easter attack in England by the IRA's top sniper.

The deadly "Jackal," armed with one of the Provos' most feared weapons, sneaked in eight weeks ago. The terrorists are believed to be planning an Easter "spectacular." And top political and military figures have been warned

that they could be targets for the assassin's long-range rifle, the Barrett Light 50, which has already claimed at least nine lives in Ulster.

The sniper alert came as the Provos issued a chilling Easter warning that their campaign of terror goes on.

● Full story – Pages 4&5

TOMORROW

3 FREE GOES AT £25m EASTER ROLLOVER

+PLUS+

£100,000

Julie's Instant Scratch Game

PLAY TODAY – PAGE 40

THAT'S IT!

FAREWELL VOYAGE: Gary, Howard, Jason with camera and Mark yesterday   Picture CHRIS GREVE

Fans in tears as Take That say goodbye

HEART-THROBS Take That sailed off yesterday in a farewell performance awash with tears.

The unlikely venue for their swansong was a tiny TV studio outside Amsterdam—and they began their journey there by riverboat.

Two thousand weeping fans besieged their hotel to say goodbye to the chart stars with eight No.1 hits. Jason Orange captured the scenes on video camera.

By MATTHEW WRIGHT

but there was deeper emotion to follow for him, lead singer Gary Barlow, Mark Owen and Howard Donald.

A technical hitch in the studio persuaded Gary to begin a spontaneous solo version of their latest hit How Deep Is Your Love.

His three pals joined in and so did the fans. "There wasn't a dry eye in the house," said one onlooker.

● Full story – Pages 2&3

Above and left: Water under the bridge as the boys give their final public performance in Amsterdam, Holland, and take in the sights on a canal taxi

DAILY Mirror

COMMENT

Kick out quango fat cats

HERE'S a gravy train that thoroughly deserves de-railing.

For years fat cats have been grabbing huge salaries for minimal work on unelected public bodies.

They are known as quangos — which in many cases translates as a free ride at the taxpayer's expense.

The situation is so out of control that the Government does not know how much is spent on quango salaries.

Even the number of quangos is in doubt. It could be 1,200, or it could be nearer 10,000.

Only three Whitehall departments publish details of their quango budgets.

The rest are spending millions of pounds of taxpayers' money without being publicly accountable.

So much for open Government.

Thankfully, there are some quango members who work hard, sometimes for no pay.

If every quangocrat followed this example, there would be no need for reform.

But there are more than enough rotten apples to justify trashing the entire barrel and starting again.

One option that must be examined is scrapping the fat-cat salaries of the quango bosses.

It's not as if they need the money — many work for quangos only a few days a year, while raking in big salaries from their full-time jobs.

They should sit on public bodies out of a sense of public duty, and not just to get their hands in the public purse.

Scrapping pay would bring another bonus. It would mean the Government could not pay off its cronies with first-class tickets on the gravy train.

Just the job, Tony

TONY Blair's visit to the United States has kicked-off on exactly the right note.

American business leaders needed to know that Britain under a Labour Government would be a safe bet for investments.

They wanted reassurance that companies would not be taxed out of business.

And they got it.

Tax rates would be internationally competitive, the Labour leader promised.

He vowed to encourage wealth creators and not hammer middle-income earners.

It was music to the ears of the financiers who have the power to bring countless jobs to Britain.

In Blair, they have found a man they can do business with.

FINAL THOUGHT

Marina's lost her buoy.

Robbie hurt us all .. but we were afraid to call him 'd***head'

NO MORE MR NICE GUY: Gary's attack will shock fans

BY RICHARD WALLACE

EXCLUSIVE Gary Barlow tells of the secret feud behind Take That split

TAKE That's Mr Nice Guy Gary Barlow has launched an astonishing attack on ex-member and pal Robbie Williams.

"He's hurt us," says Gary, "but until now we were afraid to say 'Robbie, you're a d***head, f****** get it together'."

Fab Five mastermind Gary, who is now embarking on a solo career, describes Robbie as a "loose cannon" who always hated the band's music.

Gary, 25, had remained diplomatic about Robbie's departure from the band — until now.

But his impatience with Robbie's constant public sniping prompted him to hit back.

"I'm disappointed in Robbie," says Gary. "He said he was a prisoner in Take That, that we've never been friends.

"It's complete rubbish. We're all close and always have been."

Gary says bad boy Robbie began playing up months before finally leaving the band.

"We were doing dance routines on stage but Robbie started doing his own thing.

"He'd missed out on his teenage years and wanted to live them now. He had a following of really trendy people — not the sort of people we'd ever been friends with.

"Every other week he'd be in the paper coming out of a club with a girl on his arm. That wasn't our image. There wasn't a rule book, but we'd always been aware of of what we could and couldn't do.

"There was no scandal, no

FAB FIVE: Jason, Robbie, Gary, Howard and Mark before split
Picture: PHILIP OLLERENSHAW

wild parties. When we arrived it was beautiful — nice wave, do the gig and we were home."

But not for Robbie: "We said to him 'Cool it', but he was a complete rebel.

I DON'T think he ever liked our music and he hated tours because it meant he couldn't stay up until six in the morning.

"It was all coming to a head round about the time of the Glastonbury festival in June last year when we heard he'd been on stage with Oasis. That was shocking."

It was then that Robbie revealed he wanted to quit the

band in six months. The rest of the group — Gary, Jason Orange, Howard Donald and Mark Owen — tried to dissuade him, but when he refused to change his mind he was ordered to go at once.

Gary and Robbie last saw each other at the MTV awards in Paris three months ago.

"I found myself staring at a different person," Gary tells the May edition of *Arena* magazine. "His hair and his ears were different. He wasn't the person I'd spent four years with."

Gary says Robbie, 22, thought the group would lose fans after his departure. "He was convinced we would never do it

without him. That's when the bitterness set in," says Gary. But I'm not angry at Robbie. He's just involved with the wrong sort of people. He needs to make a f***** record."

That is what Gary is about to do. His solo album, *Open Road*, is set for release shortly.

But the pop genius says he was treated shoddily by the rest of the band.

"I was a bit of an afterthought," he claims. "I was the last one the stylist bought clothes for because I never looked that good.

"I was the fat one, pushed to one side so they could get a shot of Mark and Robbie. The only thing I could shout about was the music."

GARY admits he is afraid of his fans: "It worries me that if I stop and talk someone is going to bring a knife out."

And he reveals he is hounded by paedophiles who are obsessed by the youngsters who idolise him.

"There are girls under 14 outside my house until one in the morning. And wherever our fans go, this network of perverts goes too.

"If I move house it's on the local TV news. I ring them up and say 'Thanks very much'."

Now looking for a quieter life, Gary hopes to settle down with his dancer girlfriend Dawn Andrews, 23.

"I don't think I ever communicated with any of my girlfriends before Dawn," he admits. "I don't remember having a decent chat with any of them."

Last night, Robbie's spokesman, Andrew Coulson, was unavailable for comment.

Above: Gary hits back at Robbie for his public sniping as he prepared to release his first solo album, 'Open Road'

Robbie prepares to host the 1996 MTV Europe Music Awards in November

MTV MUSIC TELEVISION®

EUROPE MUSIC AWARDS 199

TAKE TWO

After Take That split, Jason Orange modelled Manchester City merchandise in an official catalogue. He wore T-shirts and sweat pants on behalf of the club he supports.

I want Rob to be a hit

Tuesday, July 2, 1996

Gary Barlow has wished Robbie Williams good luck – despite a string of venomous personal attacks by his former Take That pal.

"I can't believe some of the things Robbie said," Gary says. "He's spoken so much rubbish."

Robbie's most recent outburst came in the glossy gay mag Attitude where he referred to Gary as "selfish, stupid and greedy".

Gary admits such slurs have hurt him deeply, but the gifted songwriter is big enough to forgive and forget, recognising his old friend's talent.

"Robbie was my friend for five years. I really loved him and I want him to make a hit record.

"Robbie was the best performer in Take That. If people were to see him on stage, he would blow them away.

"I want to hear him sing and give me goose pimples, like he used to. No matter what he has done, Robbie's talent will outshine all of it."

Gary's generosity masks the hurt he has suffered at Robbie's hands.

"He was going on about being a 'prisoner for six years in Take That'. What the hell was all that about?

"Ring someone at Strangeways and ask them if being in a pop band is like being in prison. I don't show my emotions a lot but that really upset me.

"We invested a lot in Rob. When he joined the group he was overweight and he couldn't learn the dance routines but we stood by him, we helped him and we've been nothing but faithful.

"But I'm still here and when he turns back into the Rob I knew and loved, I'll be here again.

"If he ever hits rock bottom or if he ever wants anything, then I would give it to him and I hold my hand on my heart when I say that.

"He's a bit of a time-bomb at the moment and the last thing he needs is me ringing him up.

"When the time's right, we'll meet again. Definitely."

WHAT HAPPENED TO THE LIKELY LADS

THERE WAS HUGE INTEREST IN THE FUTURE PLANS OF THE BOYS AFTER TAKE THAT CAME TO AN END. GARY BARLOW SEEMED DESTINED FOR LASTING FAME BUT ROBBIE WILLIAMS ECLIPSED THEM ALL BY EMBARKING ON A REMARKABLY SUCCESSFUL SOLO CAREER

During the 10 years that Take That were apart, the group's members headed in different directions and experienced contrasting fortunes.

Gary Barlow, the musical leader, was the one expected to prosper and enjoyed initial success with his first solo album 'Open Road', which featured two number one singles.

However, the follow-up, 'Twelve Months, Eleven Days' only reached 35 in the UK album charts and he was dropped by his record company.

Barlow went on to write songs for other artists, including Dame Shirley Bassey, Charlotte Church and Will Young. He married Take That dancer Dawn Andrews in 2000 and the couple have three children.

Robbie Williams, the first to break away from the band, enjoyed the greatest fame and fortune, despite a turbulent personal life blighted by drink and drugs problems.

The release of 'Angels' in late 1997 catapulted him to superstardom and he went on to produce a succession of hit singles and albums.

Including those won with Take That, Williams has amassed 16 Brit Awards, more than anyone else, and is said to have sold over 55 million albums worldwide. The height of his success was probably reached in 2003 when he played three consecutive shows at Knebworth that were watched by 375,000 people.

His most recent albums have met with a mixed reception but he remains one of Britain's foremost pop acts and received the Outstanding Contribution to British Music award at the 2010 Brits.

Mark Owen had solo success with the singles 'Child' and 'Clementine' but gradually faded from the public consciousness until he won the second series of Celebrity Big Brother in 2002.

Jason Orange turned to acting and played DJ Brent Moyer in the Lynda La Plante Channel 4 thriller 'Killer Net' in 1998. After a theatre role the following year, Orange travelled across Asia and Europe before going on to study a range of subjects at South Trafford College.

Howard Donald worked as a DJ and had success in mainland Europe, particularly Germany. He continues in this role when not busy with Take That.

Whatever the boys achieved, though, they were always better together than apart…

Robbie Williams performing at
Slane Castle in Ireland in 1999

Above: A huge crowd gather at Slane Castle in Ireland to see Robbie Williams. The other images show Jason publicising his acting career, Gary and Howard on stage in Hyde Park in 1998 and Mark Owen after he won Celebrity Big Brother in 2002

MAY
Gary Barlow registers his second solo number 1 with Love Won't Wait

JUNE 7
Gary's Open Road enters the UK album charts. It reaches number 1 and stays on the chart for 26 weeks

2000

JANUARY 12
Gary Barlow and Dawn Andrews marry in Nevis in the Caribbean

MARCH 5
Gary appears as a hitchhiker in the 150th episode of Heartbeat on ITV

JUNE 28
News reports claim that record company BMG has dropped Gary Barlow

2003

APRIL 11
It's announced that Take That had more covers on the recently-folded Smash Hits magazine than any other band (23 in all) – the Spice Girls could only manage seven

BACK FOR GOOD

BROADCAST IN NOVEMBER
2005, THE ITV DOCUMENTARY
'TAKE THAT: FOR THE RECORD'
BROUGHT GARY, MARK,
HOWARD AND JASON
TOGETHER AGAIN FOR THE
FIRST TIME IN NEARLY 10
YEARS. THE INTEREST
GENERATED AND THE BOYS'
REKINDLED RAPPORT
PROMPTED THE
ANNOUNCEMENT OF A FULL
COMEBACK – MINUS ROBBIE
WILLIAMS

TAKE THA

EXCLUSIVE
By NICOLA METHVEN, TV Editor

Boy band ret
lift the lid on
drugs and fi

THEY were the biggest-selling boy band since
the Beatles – five likely lads who got together
in 1990 and churned out a seemingly endless
stream of hits, while pushing all the right buttons
for a generation of young females.

Take That had it all... platinum records, good looks
and millions in the bank. But behind the smiles it was a
different story – bitterness, jealousy and resentment
ensured there would be no fairytale ending.

When Robbie Williams finally stormed out in 1995, the
other four members managed to limp on for another
miserable year but things would never be the same.
Since then, superstar Robbie has only had contact with
one of his former bandmates. Until now...

An explosive new documentary has reunited Take
That for the first time and tomorrow night, viewers will
see what Robbie, Mark Owen, Jason Orange, Howard
Donald and Gary Barlow *really* think about each other.

In the show, the lads, who sold 25 million albums and
banked £5 million each, talk candidly about the girls,
the drugs, the debauched partying – and the fights.

Robbie admits that, at the height of their fame, he
was a 19-year-old alcoholic. And it becomes clear that
he has yet to bury the hatchet with manager Nigel
Martin Smith.

These days, Robbie is an international superstar and
lives in LA. Mark, who won Celebrity Big Brother in
2002, is a solo artist based in the Lake District. Jason
has stayed out of music and spends much of his time in
Ibiza. Gary continues to pen hits, is married with two
kids and lives in Cheshire, and Howard, who has a
daughter and lives in Bournemouth, is a club DJ.

Robbie says he wishes he'd done things differently.
Looking at the quiet life now enjoyed by Gary, Robbie
says: "I would swap everything I have for what he's got."

Here is a sneak preview – in their own words – of Take
That... For The Record (ITV1, tomorrow at 9pm).

mirrorfeatures@mgn.co.uk

HOT STUFF: Take
That in their heyday
– left to right,
Howard, Jason,
Gary, Mark and
Robbie

Right: The 'For
The Record'
documentary was
the catalyst for
Take That's
extraordinary
comeback

BACK AGAIN

Having lots of sex suited me

❝ I REMEMBER our manager Nigel saying "no full-time girlfriends", which suited me actually, because then I could have lots of sex with different girls. No commitment.

But I miss the adoration the most. Who wouldn't miss that? I'll always miss that. I don't miss the other parts about being in Take That but the adulation, the kids coming along and me performing... I miss that.

I've just been to watch the recent Johnny Depp movie Charlie And The Chocolate Factory.

I was sat in the cinema and it occurred to me watching it that Nigel was basically Willy Wonka, handing out five golden tickets, and we were like these five kids going to this huge factory.

It was like this other life for a while and Nigel was in control of it.

To me, the most important thing about Take That from the beginning was our personal relationships.

When I felt like we were tight among ourselves, I felt that we were kings of the world. ❞

JASON ORANGE, 35

Robbie really hurt Mark by quitting

❝ ROBBIE let Mark down when he left. I think Mark relied on Robbie a lot – he was a good friend to Mark and, yeah, I think he missed him.

In the years since then, I can honestly say I've never laid in bed wishing I was Robbie Williams.

But I guess that, seven or eight years ago, I lay in bed wishing I had his career, definitely.

We lived the life in Take That and, in some ways, I'm still living the life. We've got so much luxury around us and that's because of all that.

OK, it was really hard work and stuff but my brother's a builder and he works much harder than I do and probably will be doing for the rest of his life. Here I am, still able to enjoy music, still able to be involved in it – that's a feat on its own in this industry.

I think that we touched a lot of people and it wasn't just a generational thing either.

It started off with young girls but the parents end up listening to what the kids listen to.

My big Take That hit, Back For Good, was heaven-sent, really. I wrote it in about 15 minutes. I played it to my producer and he nearly fell off his chair.

We were also renowned for our live shows and, by the end of the band, you would see a massive cross section of people there.

I think if you asked someone in the street they'd say "nice songs, great bunch of lads and we thoroughly enjoyed it when they were together". ❞

GARY BARLOW, 34

I went to jump into the river

❝ I WAS really disappointed when the band ended. I must have felt emotional, and tired with what was happening. I already knew that the group was going to finish and I decided to walk out the hotel and go to the Thames and sit on the wall at the side.

It was a bit stupid but I was thinking of jumping in the river because of the state of my mind at the time. I was feeling very sorry for myself at that period. It probably wouldn't have killed me, though. I would have thought: "Oh Jesus, it's too cold. I'm getting out."

As far as Robbie's quitting is concerned, we found out he was on a boat in the South of France with, I think, Paula Yates and George Michael. We thought: "Well, that's how much *he* gives a sh*t."

Before the band happened, I had dreamed that I was going to be an airline pilot.

I never dreamt that I would be a pop star or even a dancer by profession. I always thought that would be a weekend thing.

Why was it me? Why wasn't it somebody else with more talent. The whole thing is just weird.

I'm always thinking about it – what I've done and whether it really happened to me. I think Take That should be celebrated. We did a lot for 90s music, especially pop music. I'm so proud of the six years that we did. I will always be proud.

If anybody said a bad word about Take That, it would upset me or disappoint me and I would definitely take issue with them. ❞

HOWARD DONALD, 37

I'd swap my fame to be settled with a wife and kids like Gary

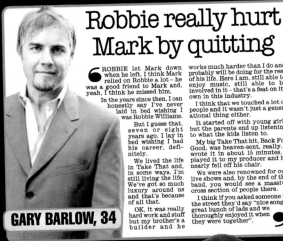

❝ MAYBE in doing this documentary I can say the right things and put a few ghosts to rest.

My drug-taking would have happened with or without Take That. Before the band I'd done acid, speed and smoked a lot of weed, so I was heading in that direction anyway. I would drink myself to oblivion every night by myself. I was so lonely.

You know I think for me, the drug intake obviously sped up a lot, until it was my life. For the other lads it wasn't really part of their life, other than we used to like to smoke weed and then giggle, we used to laugh so much. When we smoked weed we probably had the best time. Perhaps Take That saved my life. I'd have had a problem with drugs anyway.

I'd have probably been a burglar or dealer and that's the truth because I wouldn't have had the money to fund my addiction – I'd have probably been in jail now.

I must say, I don't think there's been a boy band as good as us for entertainment and for songs ever since – and you would be hard pressed to find one before, too.

I'm not talking about the Beatles – they're not a boy band – I'm talking about your archetypal 4/5 lads on stage singing and dancing.

New Kids were great and N*Sync weren't too bad but for a live show? Our shows were as good as a Madonna show, I think.

Boy bands are frigging lazy, these days. Ballad, stand, ballad, stand, when I see it, it annoys me because I know how hard we worked.

We were, and are, the best boy band that's probably ever been. ❞

ROBBIE WILLIAMS, 31

MARK OWEN, 33

It was fun and frolics

❝ SEX was something that started coming into the band more and more over the years.

The drugs, the sex and pop 'n' roll was part of what we were – we had our fair share of fun, sex and frolics.

In Spain once, we all went clubbing and did half an E or something and it was the most amazing feeling.

But there was a definite pecking order in the band – and I was near the bottom. We all did a bit of dancing and I remember Jason and Howard being really good at it, me and Rob being not so good and Gary being pretty bad. It was probably the opposite way round for the singing.

Through it all, Robbie was my mate – he made me laugh. We were both growing up together and he was my little partner in crime.

When it finished, the weirdest thing was to go from having your day-by-day schedule, then just closing the gates and going: "OK, what do I do now?" ❞

Above: Posing for photographers at the press conference where they announced they would play a series of concerts in 2006

It's official: Take That reform. Back for Good!

Saturday, November 26, 2005

They were the biggest boy-band Britain's ever seen. And now, 10 years after their split, Take That are going to relight our fires once again.

Yesterday, at a press conference at the Berkeley Hotel in London, Mark Owen thanked the thousands of readers who backed our campaign to get the boys to return for a final tour.

"Thanks so much. We loved the campaign and couldn't believe it when your email inbox was flooded by fans sending messages. You really helped us see how much public backing there still is out there."

Even though six million viewers watched their TV documentary 'Take That…For The Record' –

aired last week – and 90,000 people bought their greatest hits album in its first week, putting it at number two in the charts, Mark said it was still a difficult decision.

"We've been talking about it ever since we've started seeing more of each other again," he explained. "None of us are getting any younger, so if it's not now, it's never.

"We felt this would be the last time we can put on a show we could really be proud of – a massive spectacle."

Gary Barlow added: "When we realised how well the album's done, we knew we could play in big places.

"We'd agreed that if we couldn't play in the

right places and make it truly unbelievable, we wouldn't do it at all."

The boys are getting a bit worried about performing the physically demanding routines that made them famous.

"When we were thinking about touring we sat down and watched some of our old tour footage – I was exhausted just watching us," Mark said.

Gary is determined to get back in shape by any means necessary.

"I know I've got about a stone to lose," he admitted. "If anyone out there has any weight-loss plans, please hand them over."

Let's just Pray they shape up in time…

Below: Jason, Gary, Mark and Howard attend the premiere of the 'For The Record' documentary. Right, an advert for the 'Ultimate Tour'

2005

JANUARY
Take That meet with Sony/BMG

NOVEMBER 15
Take That go to the Coronet Cinema in Notting Hill to watch the Take That – For The Record documentary

NOVEMBER 16
Take That – For the Record airs on ITV1 and is watched by 5.7 million viewers

NOVEMBER 18
Take That appear on GMTV and Radio 2, and tape a broadcast with Jonathan Ross to air the following day on his Radio 2 show

NOVEMBER 19
Never Forget – The Ultimate Collection goes into the chart at number 2 and is kept from the number 1 spot by Madonna's album, which is released the same week

NOVEMBER 25
The band hold a press conference at the Berkley Hotel in London to announce a full comeback

THE ULTIMATE COMEBACK

TICKETS FOR TAKE THAT'S FIRST CONCERTS FOR OVER A DECADE SOLD OUT WITHIN HOURS AS THE NATION REKINDLED ITS LOVE AFFAIR WITH THE BOYS. THE RAPTUROUS RECEPTION FROM FANS LED TO A NEW ALBUM, WHICH ROCKETED THEM BACK TO THE TOP OF THE CHARTS

Howard, Gary, Mark and Jason together on stage for the first time in over 10 years

We still love Take That

Friday, May 12, 2006

They're loud, lairy and pushing 30. Age, marriage and motherhood doesn't seem to have mellowed the legion of Take That fans — if anything, it has made them crazier.

Downing alcopops and dressed to the nines tonight, they're out en masse to see their idols — and recapture the spirit of teenage years spent lusting after Gary Barlow, Mark Owen, Jason Orange, Robbie Williams and Howard Donald.

It has been a decade since the ultimate boy-band split following Robbie's rancorous departure. Their legacy of eight number one hits and 10 million album sales means they will always command a place in the UK record books and the hearts of millions of fans.

So the schoolgirls who once cried over their lyrics and screamed through their concerts have grown up and, loyally, they've never forgotten their childhood heroes.

When the band finally decided to reunite — without superstar Robbie — for what has become a 32-date UK tour, the response was overwhelming. The Daily Mirror decided to join the 14,000 not-so-young TT Army as their sell-out tour continues.

Tottering towards the MEN Arena in stilettos, pink cowboy hats and customised tops, it looks like the world's biggest — and most Bacardi Breezer-fuelled — hen night.

Mother, aunt and daughter Liz Benyon, 42, Jan, 49 and 19-year-old Amy Bonney, all from St Helens, are in the thick of the throng and have realised their long-cherished dream of seeing their idols.

"I was always a huge fan," says Liz, who works in a medical centre. "I loved Mark. I thought he was gorgeous.

"I might be older now but I still feel young at heart — as I'm sure they do."

Indeed, the band worked long and hard to recapture their youthful vigour.

They've also been stunned by the reaction they've received after such a long absence and are recording a new album.

Tickets for the shows sold out within six hours — some went on eBay for £500 — and the number of dates doubled.

Back outside the venue Aimee Burns, 25, from Cheadle, Cheshire is wondering whether she'll be making a little bit of history tonight.

She is just three weeks away from becoming a mum and sports a Take That t-shirt asking 'Who's the Daddy?'

She says: "Maybe I'll give birth tonight — it will be the first Take That baby."

While the boys are shimmying into their first outfits backstage — frilly shirts with frock-style coats — Amanda Brandariz, 24, a sales manager and her 20-year-old sister, Jo, a student, are readying their Take That-themed outfits too.

They've travelled from New Moston, near Oldham, with their mate Sarah Clark, 23, for the gig. Their TT earrings, t-shirts, scarves and even tattoos were "found at the back of a cupboard", according to Amanda.

"Back in the old days, we used to hang around where they lived," she adds. "We were obsessed. I'd send my sister to Howard's door to see if he was playing out. Not surprisingly, he never was.

"I've seen them loads of times but this is really special — because it's the one we thought would never happen and because…we can drink beer!"

Attending the Daily Mirror Pride of Britain awards in November

Top that: Comeback kings set to score double No. 1

Thursday, November 29, 2006

They are already at number one in the singles chart with their brilliant track Patience. And now Take That are on course for a stunning double as their new album heads for the top slot too.

As TT fever sweeps the country, midweek sales of their record Beautiful World have hit an impressive 43,000.

TT's high-flying chart success marks an amazing comeback for Gary, Mark, Jason and Howard. They received a rapturous reception from fans at two packed album signings in London and Manchester on Monday.

Mark Owen said: "It's like a dream. I can't believe people are still supporting us, we are just so grateful.

"It's amazing what can happen in a year. Twelve months ago I did a record signing and only 30 people showed up. Now it's thousands. This is going to be one of the best Christmases in years."

Take That the musical: TT's top tunes destined for West End show

Saturday, December 2, 2006

We had the Time Of Our Lives at Dirty Dancing, it was A Kind Of Magic at We Will Rock You – and now Take That the Musical could Relight Our Fire.

We can exclusively reveal that there are plans to stage a West End show at the end of next year. Although Mark, Gary, Jason and Howard won't be playing themselves, the show is set to be stuffed full of the boys' biggest hits.

The producers hope the Manc lads will have the final say in how the show looks and sounds.

Our theatrical mole tells us: "It's early stages but we're looking at a possible date of late 2007. Take That have a massive fan-base and their comeback over the past few months only confirms this."

We can reveal that the show hopes to follow the format of Mamma Mia – a Greek romp set to classic Abba songs – but the storyline is still to be decided.

The Super-Trouper hit is not the only musical set to a band's music – Queen show We Will Rock You, written by Ben Elton, has enjoyed a successful run since it opened in 2002.

It's been a brilliant couple of months for the Take That boys. They're on course for a double-whammy tomorrow as their new album Beautiful World heads for the top slot, and their single Patience looks set to stay at number one.

The boys have also received a rapturous reception from fans at two packed album signings in London and Manchester on Monday.

And the bandwagon rumbles on tonight with An Audience With Take That Live.

But the question on everyone's lips must be: who will play Take That on stage? Perhaps if the Boyzone reunion Louis Walsh is on about doesn't work out, they can stand in for the boys...

Above and below: Gary Barlow promotes his autobiography 'My Take'

2006

APRIL 23
The Ultimate Tour begins in Newcastle. It is the first of 29 shows which also take in Birmingham, Glasgow, Sheffield, Manchester, London, Dublin, Belfast and Cardiff

NOVEMBER 20
The band release their comeback single, Patience. It makes the number 1 spot in its second week on the UK chart

NOVEMBER 24
The comeback album, Beautiful World is released. It enters the UK album chart at number 1 and becomes one of the top 35 best-selling albums in UK music history

RULING THE WORLD

THE COMEBACK GATHERED MOMENTUM WITH THE 'BEAUTIFUL WORLD' TOUR PROVING AN
INSTANT SELL-OUT AND YET ANOTHER HIT RECORD BEING RELEASED – 'RULE THE WORLD'

Above: On stage at the 2007 Brits, where they won Best British Single for 'Patience'. Left, Gary is greeted by comedian Alan Carr

Robbie and Gary – "buds again"

Tuesday, August 7, 2007

Gary Barlow has described his recent meeting with Robbie Williams as "the best we've had since 1996".

Yesterday, the Mirror revealed how Gary, Rob and Mark Owen had dinner at Los Angeles's Chateau's Marmont hotel.

Confirmed Gary: "Yes, we met, had a great chat. He's really well and we're good buds again."

Performing at the Princess
Diana Memorial concert at
the newly-reopened
Wembley Stadium in July

2007

71

The 'Beautiful World Tour' opened in Belfast in October. It was described as their "sexiest live show"

72

Above: A sizzling dance routine from their 2007 tour

74

2007

That's hot: Take That open tour with their sexiest live show yet

Friday, October 12, 2007

They've always had the ability to get women all hot under the collar.

But as Take That kicked off their European tour in Belfast last night, things were practically xxx-rated.

Gary, Mark, Jason and Howard — whose toned bods proved they have been working out — have upped the raunch factor in their steamiest show yet.

It included an especially sizzling scene where the lads were treated to an erotic lapdance.

One of the lingerie-clad dancers who strutted their stuff during 'It Only Takes A Minute' was Gary Barlow's 33-year-old missus, Dawn. Yet she was dancing for Howard! No, we can't work that one out either.

Then the tables were sensationally turned with the girls ripping off most of the boys' clothes with Take That doing the lapdancing for them in return.

The sexy scenes had the mainly female 18,000-strong crowd whooping in delight.

Relight my attire

Monday, October 1, 2007

Here is the first picture of Take That in their latest role as models for Marks & Spencer (below).

The lads' smouldering, sharp-suited look is a world away from the happy-go-lucky boyband style of their early '90s heyday.

Jason Orange, Gary Barlow, Mark Owen and Howard Donald reformed Take That last year, a decade after they broke up.

It has paid off, with a hit album and tour and now this high-profile advertising deal, revealed by the Mirror last month.

One marketing insider said: "Take That fans who grew up with the group are now probably married or in steady relationships.

"They are the wives and girlfriends who will want to buy those clothes for their partners."

Left: Howard Donald arrives at the premiere of 'Stardust', the film for which Take That wrote and recorded 'Rule The World'. Above, the boys model for Marks & Spencer and, below, picking up a Mirror 3am award

76

RECORD BREAKERS

THE SECOND COMEBACK ALBUM, 'THE CIRCUS', RELEASED IN 2008, WAS ANOTHER HUGE SUCCESS AND SPAWNED A SPECTACULAR TOUR THE FOLLOWING YEAR

TAKE TWO

Gary Barlow was said to have developed an aversion to ballet pumps and banned crew members from wearing them backstage during the Circus tour.

Top: Accepting another award at the 2008 Brits, while (right) the group line up at London's St Pancras Station ahead of a trip to Paris to promote The Circus album

Call me, Gary

Friday, March 27, 2009

Robbie Williams is waiting for a call from Gary Barlow to seal one of pop's most eagerly-awaited reunions.

The Angels singer, 35, broke his silence to confirm for the first time that he hopes to rejoin Take That.

He said: "Let's see what happens, but my head's in the right place, so the timing could be right if Gary calls. I think it would be fun."

Robbie also revealed his old bandmates want him back for good and went on: "I'm in regular contact with them, even Gary, so it's looking more likely by the week.

"The lads seem up for it and some people think it's a done deal. It would make sense for it to happen some time over the next year."

He assured fans the feud that followed his 1995 departure was over. "We've matured now. We'd have a laugh."

Gary, Mark Owen, Jason Orange and Howard Donald split in 1996 but reformed in 2005 and have since sold six million albums. Gary hinted last December that they would perform again with Robbie, as he said: "We will one day. I just don't know when."

Above: Robbie reveals that he would welcome a reunion

Below: Mark takes in the acclaim from the adoring crowd during The Circus tour

2008

FEBRUARY 9
Take That win two more Brit Awards for Best British Live Act and Best British Single for Shine

MAY 22
The band win an Ivor Novello Award for Most Performed Work with Shine

NOVEMBER 24
Greatest Day, the first single from the album The Circus, is released and goes straight in at number one on the UK Singles chart – the band's 11th UK chart-topper

DECEMBER 1
The Circus is released, debuting at number one and remaining there for five weeks

2009

MARCH 2
Up All Night, the second single from The Circus, is released. It peaks at number 14 on the UK Singles chart

JUNE 15
Said It All is released as a single and goes on to reach number 9

JUNE 5
Take That start their The Circus Live tour at the Stadium of Light in Sunderland. The run ends on July 5 and becomes the fastest-selling of all time, with 650,000 tickets selling in under four-and-a-half hours

NOVEMBER
Take That release the official DVD of their Circus tour, which becomes the fastest-selling music DVD of all time in the UK on its first day of release. The previous best was the DVD of the band's own Beautiful World Live tour

NOVEMBER 23
Take That release their first live album Take That Present: The Circus Live which sells 98,000 copies on its first day of release and is certified platinum the following month

In their most spectacular tour to date, Take That hold the crowd in the palm of their hands while performing at the Ricoh Arena, Coventry, in June.

Rewrite my fire

Monday, September 28, 2009

Robbie Williams has embraced one of the most talked about reunions in pop history in a studio on the other side of the Atlantic.

The star seems to have buried the hatchet with his old Take That mates and it is believed they are back working on songs together.

The boys had arranged to meet in New York for Mark Owen's stag do. But they also had a hush-hush reunion on Saturday and Sunday at the Electric Lady Studios, built for Jimi Hendrix.

It is the first time all five have been at work together as a group since Robbie left to pursue a solo career in 1995.

Robbie flew from Los Angeles to New York with his girlfriend, American actress Ayda Field, on Wednesday. That night he joined Mark, Gary Barlow, Howard Donald and Jason Orange for dinner.

They got on brilliantly during the boozy get-together over steak and chips at private members' club Soho House.

On Saturday they joined forces again as a band – ending 14 years of separation.

Robbie, 35, was spotted arriving at the studio, in Manhattan's West Village, at 2.30pm. The other four left together with a bodyguard at 9.20pm and walked back to Soho House, where they are believed to be staying.

And the boys were back at the studio yesterday, Robbie arriving at 2.15pm – two hours after first arrivals Gary and Howard. The band are putting the finishing touches to a forthcoming live album but are expected to write new songs with Robbie.

Above: Robbie is snapped entering the same New York recording studio as the rest of the boys in September 2009. It later emerges that all five were working on songs for a new Take That album

Left: Gary Barlow and Robbie Williams reunited on stage for the Children In Need concert at the Royal Albert Hall in November

ROBBIE RETURNS: IT'S OFFICIAL

AFTER YEARS OF RUMOURS, ROBBIE WILLIAMS'S RETURN TO TAKE THAT WAS FINALLY CONFIRMED IN JULY. TIME WILL TELL IF HE IS BACK FOR GOOD

2010

JUNE 7
Robbie Williams's website reveals news of a new single called Shame which was written by and features the vocals of both Gary Barlow and Williams. The single is to be included on Williams's new greatest hits album In and Out of Consciousness which is due for release in October 2010. It is the first time the two have worked with each other for 15 years.

JULY 15
The news we'd all been waiting for finally arrives: Robbie has rejoined Take That. A new album is to be released in November, with a tour to follow.

Right: Together again – the boys are pictured outside a London studio, while putting the finishing touches to their new album

I AM
▶ Robbie back in band

ROCK & STROLL Lads walk tall after reunion

BANTER Rob and the boys take time for a joke during recording

OCT 1990 Nigel Martin-Smith picks the band members.
JUNE 1992 First single It Only Takes a Minute peaks at No 7 in UK charts.
AUG First album, Take That

and Party, spawned four UK No 1 singles – Pray, Relight My Fire, Babe and Everything Changes.
FEB 1993 Brit Award for Best Single, Could it be Magic.

2010

ROBBIE'S BACK

3am EXCLUSIVE
BY **CLEMMIE MOODIE**
clemmie.moodie@mirror.co.uk

HOME

He'll open dates on huge tour

HE quit under a cloud of acrimony, but after 15 years of going it alone Robbie Williams is back with the band that launched him on the road to fame.

And the 36-year-old described the reunion as like "coming home" from a solo career that has lurched between brilliance and despair.

It is a homecoming that will net the singer £6million with a new album and 50-date tour next summer – a move that will delight millions of fans.

Robbie joined up with bandmates Gary Barlow, 39, Jason Orange, 40, Howard Donald, 42, and 38-year-old Mark Owen at a studio in West London yesterday to put the finishing touches to their as yet unnamed CD.

The move confirms the Mirror's exclusive story in a March 2009 interview with Robbie that the band were getting back together. Robbie said last night: "I get embarrassingly excited when the five of us are in a room. It feels like coming home."

Mark added: "Getting the five of us to be in a room together, although always a dream, never actually seemed like becoming a reality.

"Now the reality of the five of us making a record together feels like a dream.

"It's been an absolute delight spending time with Rob again."

A source said of the studio session: "The boys spent hours reminiscing and listening to the new tracks.

"Everything is a joint decision on this album. They all wanted to be together to finalise the track listing before it was released to the world. They are really happy with it."

Robbie, who went into rehab three years ago battling a terrible drug addiction, co-wrote the new album.

It is the first time they have recorded a full one together since the release of Nobody Else in 1995.

Along with gigs and merchandise, it is set to earn the boys £4.2million each, with an extra £2million for main songwriters Gary and Robbie.

The album is being produced by Stuart Price, the man behind Madonna's last work. The group will begin preparations for a gruelling tour, headlining at Wembley or the O2.

Promoters AEG are understood to be in a bidding war, trying to secure a residency at the O2 in London. Tour sponsorship and branding could see the band further line their pockets.

It is understood Robbie will open each gig, followed by the others performing their own tracks. All five will unite for the finale, singing a mixture of old and new material.

But while the news was music to the ears of many who longed to see the old line-up back together again, not everyone was enthralled by the idea of Stoke-born Robbie's return.

One fan forum even started a thread called "Who hates Robbie Williams?" while others questioned the singer's motives for returning.

Many believe Take That should remain a foursome – a formula that has brought them unprecedented success since they got back together in 2005.

While Robbie remained holed up in LA with fluctuating success as a solo artist – and a major drug problem – Take That secured two number one platinum albums, including The Circus, the fastest selling record of 2008. Last year's spectacular arena tour was also the fastest selling series of concerts in British history.

The band's reunion ends months of speculation over whether or not all five of them will ever perform again. It follows cameo get-togethers at a Children In Need concert in November with Gary introducing old enemy Robbie onto the stage. The pair had a very public falling over the split.

The boys met up in New York last autumn for Mark's stag do. While there they spent time in the studio, working on six tracks for the new album. It was also announced last month that Robbie and Gary co-wrote a track, Shame, to be released in October that will feature on Robbie's greatest hits album.

When Take That, who have sold more than 80 million records, announced their split in 1996, a Samaritans hotline was set-up for traumatised teens.

During their boyband career, they had 17 number one singles, played live to more than 14.5 million people and won 19 Brit awards. They first sang live as a group 20 years ago on nightclub TV show The Hitman & Her.

Voice of the Mirror: Page 8

▲ **IN HARMONY** Gary and Robbie at Royal Albert Hall in November

8I

By GAVIN MARTIN
Mirror music critic

WHY on earth, after staging one of the most unexpectedly successful comebacks in recent memory, would the remaining Take That members want to get back with Robbie Williams?

Only recently has Williams – with his career on the slide – had warm words for the band he left in the lurch in 1995.

But in making up with Robbie, Take That have completed the PR makeover they began in 2005 with the award-winning For The Record documentary.

They have managed to do precisely what boy bands aren't supposed to – grow up.

And expect plenty of sold-out gigs, making it an astute move commercially for all five.

By BETH NEIL
Mirror Take That fan

THEY'D been hinting at it so long I'd almost died of boredom.

Yes, the return of Robbie to Take That has been on the cards for ages – ever since the other four got their mojo back and he went a bit rubbish, in fact.

As a former Take That diehard, I'm chuffed to bits to see the boys back together. Seeing them on stage as a five piece is going to turn a generation of 30-something women into a seething hormonal mass of lust, sweat and tears.

It'll be like Whitley Bay Ice Rink 1994 all over again.

I just hope Robbie doesn't try to steal the limelight and over-shadow the other four, who have grafted non-stop to become the nation's biggest man band.

◄ **BONDING** Boys say it's a dream to have Robbie back

◄ **THUMBS UP** Rob is delighted to be back in studio

4:48:57 14/07/2010 Unit 01

Third album, ...se. Sure is UK ...for Good tops ...l countries. ...ie Williams ...p. Almost ...on drugs.

AUG-OCT First world tour. Win Best Live Act at MTV Europe Awards.
FEB 1996 Take That announce they are disbanding.
NOV 2005 Reunite for the ITV documentary Take That: For the Record.
MAY £3million recording deal with Polydor Records is announced.
APRIL 'Final' show performed in Amsterdam.
JUNE 2006 Sell-out Ultimate Tour starts. Comeback album Beautiful World enters chart at No 1.
FEB 2007 Brit Award for single Patience.
OCT Beautiful World Tour starts in Belfast.
NOV 2008 Single Greatest Day, from The Circus album debuts at No 1. Band on TV's X Factor as finalists sing their hits.
DEC Robbie says he won't go back and needs to focus on his solo career.
JUNE 2010 New single Shame co-written by Barlow and Williams. Robbie says he will rejoin Take That for one year.

DAILY Mirror

Friday
July 16, 2010

REAL NEWS.. REAL ENTERTAINMENT 45p

SORRY: MOTHER BEHIND 'MOAT IS LEGEND' WEBSITE

PAGE 7

Wazza fills his boots

HE GETS £40K A WEEK RISE.. & WINS £4.5M COURT FIGHT

PAGE 11 & SPORT

▶ **TOGETHER** Take That are reunited in London studio

RETAKE THAT!

By CLEMMIE MOODIE

THIS is the picture that will delight millions of Take That fans – Robbie Williams back with the band as they prepare to release an album and embark on a string of gigs.

The 36-year-old singer reunited with Gary Barlow, Jason Orange, Mark Owen and Howard Donald 15 years after quitting amid a series of rows in 1995.

Robbie is expected to land £6million from the new songs and a 50-date UK tour. He joined the boys at a recording studio in West London to put the finishing touches to their album.

Mark said: "Our dream has become a reality." Robbie said he was "excited" at the reunion, exclusively revealed by the Mirror last year.

FULL STORY: PAGES 4&5

▲ **HEYDAY** Band before Robbie quit in 1995

▶ **Robbie earns £6million to get back with the lads after 15 years**

▶ **New album, 50-date tour, they say 'our dream is reality'**

Above: The front page of the Daily Mirror from July 16 as the full line-up are reunited for the first time in 15 years

82